A Drink

Called

Paradise

A Drink

Called

Paradise

A Novel

Terese Svoboda

COUNTERPOINT

WASHINGTON, D.C.

Copyright © 1999 by Terese Svoboda

Library of Congress Cataloging-in-Publication Data
   A drink called paradise : a novel / Terese Svoboda.
      p.   cm.
   ISBN 1-58243-001-2 (acid-free paper)
   I. Title.
PS3569.V6D75   1999
813'.54—dc21   99-12664
                                                          CIP

Jacket, jacket art, and book design by Amy Evans McClure

Printed in the United States of America on acid-free paper that meets the American National Standards Institute Z39-48 Standard.

COUNTERPOINT
P.O. Box 65793
Washington, D.C. 20035-5793

Counterpoint is a member of the Perseus Books Group.

10 9 8 7 6 5 4 3 2 1

To Pat Heller

This time the islanders seem determined to
let somebody else be the guinea pig.

*Bob Payne, "Diving with
Bikini's Ghosts,"* Condé Nast/Traveller

Acknowledgments

Thank you Molly Giles, Esther Figueroa, Sondra Olsen, William Melvin Kelley, Jay Hartwell, Donald Sutherland, the Pukapukans I met on Rarotonga, and my dear Steve Bull.

_._._._._._._ *Part 1*

Ah, sex. That's the subtext of roosters, all roosters. What could be more compelling than the undertones of sex on a desert island, an atoll exactly, with a blood-hot climate and a flame-headed fury of a rooster strutting around the thick uprightness of a coconut palm?

But is this all it is?

Barclay pronounces his lying *yes,* his polite lying *yes,* along with its denial of the rest of my life, and it could just as well be the rooster's *yes.*

What he means is he's ready.

Ready or not, I read it to mean.

That is the least of it.

I have a tan, but I am white enough. In books they write that people here stay indoors for weeks to get my color, that this is the color of love they wait for. I am also blond, although that is soon taken care of, day by day, a quarter-inch at a time. I see how the water moves each wave to leave a rope of the darkened sand, and that's my hair, its true self, not saying *sex* or *foreign* or the two, inevitably, together.

A week on an island is a wonder. A week after missing a boat is a reprieve, time to fix it in your head, every stripe in the sunset, everything last, last, last. It's the next week that sticks in your throat when you try to forget how long it is, then you do and you go on to the next week, you can't help but hear that *yes* Barclay makes, its crow. If weeks can be gone through like days, one as warm and wet as the next, then they're not long, then there's no worry, take a *yes*.

Missing the boat is not a worry, it is a dumb thing. Ngarima says there is a spear I must see like all the rest that I must see before I leave: the taro pits, the shells ivory smooth, the way you beat bark, but the boat is coming in, is coming close. Don't worry, she says, it is only for a minute, over here, she says. I worry, but she has seen many boats, she knows. Come over here, she says. It's seven foot long, she says. The most beautiful, she says, the one more thing.

The day before the day before the next time the boat should come, it rains in a release like a latch broken, and then it rains the week away, and then the next. Here lashes the tail of a typhoon and the typhoon's brother and what else? I worry. Rain and its typhoon approach or Barclay's can make you worry. Today it's rain-you-can't-lift-your-hand-in. All you're allowed in this kind of rain is one foot in front of the other, and only just before the other foot disappears.

Barclay has disappeared.

Oh, I make a scene when I miss the boat. I know by the silence after I speak, the way waves lap so loudly in between what I say. Ngarima says the boat had a problem, it had to leave quick, and Barclay says his *yes*. They can say that because of a radio. I'm sure there is a radio. I ask every day about a radio to call some other boat, a boat that might be boating by, even here, and every day Barclay says, Yes.

Today the rain drowns, literally it seems, even the rooster's fervent and urgent riffs that break from that rain-sodden swollen chest. The cuckolding of every other rooster that has ever scratched or jerked in the surrounding circle of coral ends short, recedes to mere complaint, and then to nothing, and leaves me bereft and angry.

I can't find Barclay.

He's not in either of the two rooms inside. I run out to where I last saw his large self angling. The rain closes around me in its sheaf of wet and that's all I make out until I find the porch ledge and then I'm back to where I drip on the porch.

It's an island, can he go far or forever? says Ngarima. He has gone for sex is what I think, sex outside this sandwich we don't make here, and not to any radio if there is one. It isn't a boat he cares about, it's sex elsewhere, and my sex just sitting here, missing and waiting.

I could plunge back into the rain and search the length of the rain for him, but why not wait now and believe his *yes?* Tourists wait and are waited on. Why not wait a week longer with my anger and no boat? There are no boats in a typhoon anyway, and there is probably no radio. The lack of truth is what makes me angry, all its *yes* promise.

All Ngarima promises now is food. No, that is not all she promises. Like Barclay, she is a connoisseur of promising, but today she heaves her huge self out onto the porch with a piece of taro the size of a country ham and a machete tucked, as only an islander can tuck a knife, under her arm, then she settles, a dark enough cloud herself, not a yard away from me.

The rain waggles. It could be a ghost, it could be a skirmish of hot and cold, it could be wind from Oklahoma out to lunch or a long shot slapped down right here in the middle of the Pacific. But most likely ghost.

If she could talk over this rain, Ngarima would tell me ghost, the way she would tell me the kind of day this is for cooking or the size of the fish no one caught so there is just this can of fish to eat. She doesn't show me this and that anymore, all that is finished with missing the boat as if missing the boat were why she showed me everything, but she still talks ghost. Ghosts lounge around here like everybody else. If she sneezes, there's a ghost, if she finds a roach in with the food, a ghost stuck it there. After her ghost answer, she would ask if I have children because she likes that question, that's a question I can't answer well enough. The question sounds like one an anthropologist would ask over and over, as if there were another answer. Then she would ask if I like sex, as if it is something we are having for dinner. Or as if Barclay is having me.

Barclay does like his service. Along with his name, which he took from something washed up, a biscuit tin or a sailor, he has that stealthy, passive, tilted pelvis when he speaks down to the seated Ngarima, and a washed-up wave of dark hair that cuts off his face while he talks. That face is a film star's, good eyebrows and chin—you could *yes* him—but a look on the features says whatever sailor made that slim nose in the smallest part of his person left for good reason, and the colors of his logoed T-shirt scream so ugly I'm frightened for fashion, whatever it took to get it this far.

All tourists think their island's far, but this island's really far. You can't fly in—you have to take a boat. There isn't even a brochure. I'm in ads, and a place without a brochure is some secluded place. I just stumbled onto it, hustling a soft drink I copywrote Paradise, which meant the drink needed an island better than where the fruit came from to shoot its ad in, in fact, the place we found wasn't clean enough either, too many rocks on the beach, a lot of beer webbing and mangrove and guano, so we had to get on another plane, and once I got there, what is one more island, one more week away by boat?

Crazy, the crew said. But I have spent the last six months moving six words into as many orders as six words will go—I know crazy. To be sure, my ticket had to be cleared. Someone looked at my ticket and then someone else looked at it, they both stamped it *okay* to show how they both looked, and then they looked at each other as if I were getting away with what?

Paradise.

Not that I don't love ad life. Writing something from nothing is important in these days of few blue skies, no water clean enough to spit in, and no place to drive that Malibu four-wheel sheet-metal bomber that ad life said would take you. That I said would.

It's the romance of the thing I know how to write: the bent palm, the burn of a cigarette in the dark, pearls against a tawny neck, water reflections, most of what started here and was whispered, sailor to merchant to whore to chamberlain to some philosopher walking around a big lake in a cold country who made romance what it is so I can remake it, wrap dollars around it so people can burn their lives away answering yes.

Ngarima takes her machete out from her armpit and sections the big, thick taro in her lap into three huge chunks, all white through, all gray-brown rough outside, then she pares it, hacks at it until its gray-brown outsides curl at her knees.

This is what island life is really like: knives and rain. How else will you have growth? It is a mistake to think sex, that romance, and not to see how this kind of growth is part of it. Plants knife the rain at the end of the porch, waggle in the violent wind, shake with a drop in temperature or when a ghost moves the plant's long, slender leaves—everything here is so stiff and ready to cut or come, it's sex and death together. On this island you can see right where those two end: in a circle, curved, according to all the theories, curved and meeting at the edges with ocean.

I'm on this island until the end of time. Not so terrible, you say. Relax, you say. A few extra weeks on an island, what's the big deal? Those days of speed-dialing and demanding, with no time for food, for love, the present never present I am so nervous with fade to static now under this sun, under this lack of sun. No doubt there is a Zen lesson here, a long lesson, but one that lacks the amusing riddle.

Maybe you think I exaggerate. Maybe you think the end of time is quite impersonal, Cretaceous or Pleistocene only with some future suffix, but I know the world and its end are inextricably linked to my personal decay, so that when I finish with the world in whatever hole I've stolen from somebody else, via some ad or other, time will simply perish because I am time. Bury me now and carbon dating will tell.

The rain keeps falling. Ngarima and I stare into the gray, we listen to how the tin roof bangs back with the hard parts of the rain so we can't possibly talk. We sleep instead, sleep without going to all the trouble of closing our eyes.

The water that falls, parts. A helmet parts it. The top of the helmet says *Green Bay Packers* as it parts the water in a line straight toward us. The helmet's approach makes Ngarima squeal and clutch her machete, her open-eyed sleep severed and over. Does she squeal from shock, the helmet running from dream to her porch, or has he come for sex, his small wet self an offering, and there I am in the way, with my flat-out Europeanness a flag of missionarydom despite my grown-out blond hair, my too-short shorts and halter?

But he is the missionary. Ngarima issues an order to her boy, who abandons the roach toy he has brought to the porch's edge, a roach coach and harness or a roach airplane, a pink cast-off thread from my shorts tying the three roaches together so they can still fly, and the boy rouses himself, but before he leaves he addresses the helmeted man Preacher. I know that address from my week of touristing the tumbledown this and that in bright colors at odd angles that dot the croissant that keeps the palms upright. Crescent, not croissant. The carnal inverts even the words here. So the man runs a church, but which one is not plain because there's only a paper cross in one window.

In the break in the rain—brought on by the helmet's cleaving?—I ask after the preacher's church.

Latter Day sounds right for here, nearly postmodern, with Christ rising again in no time or at least in our time, whenever we can agree on what time while time is stopped like this. He runs a mission not a church because he finds his own food, his own cinder blocks and paper cross, while Latter Day just sends the paper. They do do that.

The dripping helmet rocks on the porch floor between us. Cheerleading, concussions, crisp fall burnt leaves, and school bunting power through my brain, as far away in time as in place. I touch its dome, I mime a why? through the pounding rain.

The missionary points at the wisps of hair plastered to his skull like the strands on a husked coconut and bends that skull toward me so I can see a brown scar slashed where a crack might be. He then points to the closest palm and its load, which waves and shakes, suddenly slingshot.

No porch-leaving for me.

From inside, the boy brings out Milo, a substitute of a substitute for coffee but the real thing here, and for me the heat above the cup, which exceeds the heat of the rain, is fiercely and unexpectedly refreshing. I drink it.

We all stare at the rain.

My eyes burn from the hour I must have left them open, not knowing I wasn't awake. The gray, unflinching curtain continues like the inside of eyelid but solid and noisy in downpour. Even the inside of the missionary's helmet is wet, and now a slight shift in the rain's direction sprays us all an inch closer together.

Will the boat come? I ask. Do you have a radio?

The missionary gives me his *yes,* his *no.*

We sit together for a long time, not speaking. I sense they don't speak because I am present, although they could speak in their island way, but they don't. But I don't retreat. The porch holds what little light there is, and besides, inside sits Ngarima's son, training more roach horses, letting them fly.

It is more a kind of hesitation that the man and Ngarima have by not speaking or not leaving. It is not me, my presence. And it's not a liaison I'm preventing. He and his cracked head, his missionary way of thanking the boy when he comes to collect the cups—all this doesn't add up to sex. I have been sitting on the porch too long with warm rain coming through the boards. This is not something I'm always thinking. But maybe Ngarima is looking at him when I'm not looking—or maybe it's just him, and their not talking, that makes me think they do think of sex.

Should I go inside? I ask, as if this is what they're thinking.

No is one answer, Ngarima's.

In America, asks the preacher, where the Latter Day sits, they have deserts to drive on?

You just go straight along, I nod with relief, until you're gone.

The three of us look where you could be gone, through all that water. This is no lush volcanic island, I say, despite all this rain.

An atoll, says the missionary. The story, he says, is that a young man fished the land out of the water.

Or did the sky and water use their sex? asks Ngarima.

Aha, I think, she is thinking it. But then she sighs, making the sex less, like *having relations*. No, she says, they do that later, to make a man.

The missionary strokes his scarred head. Really what makes land is all the coral animals squeezing in with each other. That makes it strong. That's the way island people are. But coral does crack, says the missionary. I have seen cracks, he says.

I'm not afraid of cracks, I say. LA could crack and fall right off, and it's not even coral.

When I mention some part of where I'm from that they don't already know about, they look off. It is as if I am telling about a dream I have, that dull, that particular. I go on thinking about all my work in LA cracking off in a quake, sliding right down into the ocean, right off into the water. Maybe it has, maybe they have already finished with Paradise, people have bought it and have quit buying it.

One drink and you think you're Eve, that's what I wrote. *If you can drink this drink, you can live in paradise* is mine too. A little snappier, but that is what it was, more or less. The war over it was: Is Paradise lemon-lime? Does it fizz? But when the bottle finally comes, who wants to drink it? Not even on the set did we drink it. We settled for water. But everybody wants the word *paradise,* it's all dollar signs.

Not pearly gates.

I sip my Milo. Without milk or sugar, it is bitter vegetable, something you would beg a child to drink, telling him how it would make him grow. I steel myself to swallow.

I can't think about children.

Ngarima's son comes out with a pleated plastic rain hat. How does he know she needs her rain hat? No words that I hear pass between them. She hands him her finished Milo cup, the preacher helps her upright, and the porch shudders.

She stands.

The small bit of pleated plastic does cover her woolly island hair well enough, but the rest of her, with the bulk of some army vehicle, something large yet still moving, sweeps into the deluge with its shoulders bare, the water sluicing and splashing around her, parting the water for the preacher behind, who has to go on into the rain for some reason, and with her.

Ngarima's boy invents a dog. At least you don't have to walk it, I say as he trains the roach to roll over.

Insects are the future, he tells me. My father says so. He knows.

What else does he know? When the boat's coming back?

The boy nods as if I don't listen. He says, He doesn't want me to go on the boat.

Parents don't want children to go anywhere.

The boy rights his cockroach, puts it back inside a shell, and plugs the shell with a rock. This will help it learn.

Where I live, I say, boys go swimming. Why don't you swim? I ask. All the time I've been on this island I've never seen you swim. The only one who swims is there.

I point to a head in the lagoon, just above the water from this angle. You can finally see the lagoon because the rain has stopped, and what you can see is what you see daily, a head, tiny like a baby's, over a big board, with long arms like a man's that go around it. When I go in, the head and arms are always gone, the board against a tree. What about that swimming? I say.

Water gets in your throat and you cough, he says. He coughs to show me. There's too much water. You see him? He doesn't need to breathe so much — look at the size of his head.

We look.

Where I live, I begin again, boys play ball or go to school or watch TV.

Here, all the balls go into the lagoon, then trade winds take them away, he says. And the school here is closed now until we get a new teacher.

He turns his shell over. You can be the teacher, you can tell us about TV.

This is how you turn it on, I say, and I twist my wrist, touch a channel. Unless you have a remote, then you just press.

Ngarima's son just presses.

I think you've got it, I say.

He presses and presses.

A pig squeals, caught on a kitchen can outside. Why doesn't anybody fish around here? I ask, after he frees it. Even if you don't eat the fish, it would pass the time.

He rattles the shell. No boats, he says.

But why aren't there any boats? These islands are famous for boats.

Nobody can buy them here.

Sure, I say. But can't you just go and make them like before?

He laughs. Who knows how? he says. He puts his hands up and out. Do you? he asks, as if I know.

Back on the porch Ngarima screeches, Come get food for us.

Ngarima's son fetches a can of mackerel from which he skinnies out all of the fish without losing its can shape. I am offered a chunk to go with a piece of taro that I still have from an earlier offering. No, no more, I say. I might as well say yes. He disturbs his cylinder with his finger, the chunk is mine no matter what, and the curls of coconut jelly he scrapes from the lid of the nut I drink from come with it.

I eat one for the other, the jelly surely a drug, so cool and smooth I want to climb back into the coconut with it. Ngarima's son eats what's left in the bottom of the can, then beats on its bottom in quick rhythms. Over at the next house, a two-year-old sways with her hips, she sways and falls down on some slick of her porch, then gets up, goes on with his beat.

How many live on this island all the time? I ask. Even if it isn't so big, I say.

Not so many as before, says Ngarima, but she doesn't say before what.

There's a book in my room, I say, that says a hundred and eighty-three. But is this the number made up for the book or the number that once was and is not now?

It's hard to count, she says. A hundred and eighty-three is not a bad number.

Ngarima's son begins counting. At the number fifteen, the two of them begin to talk about clouds of people, groups that re-form and flatten and pour into houses, regardless of cousins or whose father. The number swells and pulses, and I think of my son, my only population.

Ngarima's son has a name, but I can't repeat it the way they like to hear it, so in my head it is *son,* like Abrahamson or Jackson. No one can say my name. When they say it, it is Rare. Rare this and that, which makes me smile. I'm beginning to think I am, white where it doesn't count on an island of brown, all alone, the way all tourists, no matter how many are on an island, like to think they are. That's the way I write it: one couple, a single set of prints. I don't show the six people raking the sand behind them what allows their aloneness.

But I am not alone. Harry with his Rolex clothes, whatever wardrobe goes with the watch, waded off the lighter with me. I felt sad then for his name-brand shoes taking in so much salt. He could've pulled them off, but he was too eyes-wide, salt-be-damned. Not that I know much about him. Seasickness does that to you, and the close company of pigs. I am not fond of pigs. Prop pigs, yes. Or pigs with careers, with handlers and sixty-second contracts.

Hi, I say to him anyway when we hit the beach. He says his *hi*, but it includes a couple dozen island girls who wreathe him like a race horse.

Who thinks about people living in paradise and so far from everywhere—I mean, why would they be here? It's paradise for sure, but no one lives in paradise every day. Unless they're staff. And for staff it is never paradise, it's bookings and changing rolls in bathrooms. How can people expect to live in paradise for nothing, by just being born here?

The first thing I get on this island is a coconut, which this islander hands me, this islander who turns out to be Barclay, and I look it over like it's something he's selling.

But Barclay smiles, pure plaster saint. Over here, he waves us toward a car behind him. We two play Columbus showing up with Eric the Red, each of us making his singular discovery, each left-righting so separately toward that car. Harry throws his bag through its broken window, then tries to open the door but the handle comes off in his hand. Barclay takes it from him and tosses it over his shoulder with a laugh, to where other parts lie, maybe another whole car in pieces, and we all start walking the path beside the car, which is what will really take us.

Was I wanting a high-rise haven with matching hot towels and wraps? No, I can handle "individually appointed," even adventure, but the place we come to has been kayoed to its knees long ago and did not get up, this place has a door cut to accommodate what? A Quonset hut, all of a world war in its half-moon frame. To cheer it up, someone has set out a dozen already opened coconuts along the base, but the cheer looks more like a lot of raw, chopped-up open mouths.

Let's take a look, I say.

We make our way inside. Hmmmm, says Harry, as we pace its one room, I guess we'll have to put up a curtain.

Divorced three years, I can't see spending my week on a remote island with the only guy off the boat. Besides, what we have here is not love at first sight.

No thanks, I say.

That is how I get to be a local. All tourists want that if they want to be somewhere else. I get a bag of rice for a bed, and a lamp, but what makes my room at Barclay's so somewhere else shimmers in its one window: a beach so white, white crayon on white paper is about right, a white that stretches—yawns and stretches—its way to the lagoon of choice, the ur-lagoon of every ad for paradise. For a week I float in the amber of a good time, maybe a little lonely with nobody to sigh off into the sunset with, but I collect myself, chase children who squirt me with rubber-hose creatures that grow in the shallows, burn the continental drift into my sandy thighs, cavort with snorkel and mask in the empty lagoon.

Empty except for that tiny head on a board, swirling and stopping, swirling and stopping.

You aren't hungry? screeches Ngarima. You are sick? She's spotted my leftover portion, some of my taro hidden upright beside the can.

She feels my forehead.

The way coconut is food for pleasure, taro is punishment. The queen of starch, you can taste in every bite all the shirts it could stiffen.

I've eaten plenty, I say. I don't say, I eat small bites to parse out the taste.

Go, says Ngarima to me as if I'm her son, one of the family, as if I'll obey. Go inside and get another tin, she says.

No, no, please, I'm fine, I say.

Open the drawer there—just inside—and you'll find one. I keep them in the drawer.

Her voice tells me she won't take no.

I cross into the kitchen. She is my host, after all. I am a paying guest, but this is her house. I open the drawer next to the food safe, the one I think is the one she means, but I discover this is not the drawer, that this drawer should not be opened. There's sugar at the bottom of this drawer, an inch of it spilled on purpose, and the purpose flies up at me when I open it, out flies a flock of gold-brown roaches. I scream, and then Ngarima screams, That's their drawer.

—·—·—·—·—·—·—·—·—

I am thinking I must leave my room and cross the kitchen again, I must pass its roaring roaches, I must go out, I must go to the bathroom, I must go for a walk, I must see if the rain's truly stopped and how stopped and whether it will rain again. I am thinking how I've made my own island, how one island begets another, like a fish with an organ bag you can see through, all the seeds of future fish in a row, ready to be born and bear and be born again, when I begin to creep past the drawer, which is now closed and not still pulled out to the point where I left it, when I start picking my way past the oozing white of what flew up at me earlier, which I beat down and made ooze, and just then, while I am concentrating on getting around it all and not thinking, a man-sized boy with such a head crashes in from the porch with his arms flailing and a noise coming out of him in big gobs like something left on and stuck.

Boom—pink shredded plastic and streaks of pepper sauce and ketchup, a full jar of mayonnaise, all three of the family's forks ricochet off the kitchen walls, and its cooking pot, its charcoals and tinder, are smeared into the mess with one more whirl of his long, long arms, with one more great gob of sound.

Back, shouts Ngarima's son. Back to Auntie, go on back to Auntie. Go on.

The boy is coming for his room, my room, my room that was so empty when I came, and now I know why—those long arms pull down anything in their windmilling radius. But I'm too stunned by the boy's tiny head, let alone the whipping arms, to stop him from going into my room, to connect what has happened in the other room with those arms that whip toward my clothes, books, passport, money, ID, sun lotion—and his space.

Ngarima's son raises the boy's board, the one the boy floats on with his long arms, and he hits him with it, he tries to herd him away from the room by beating him with its hard foam. The boy falters in his furious beeline, he turns in circles beside his brother in the staccato of the beating.

His brother hits him again and again.

I do not scream, seeing the boy being beaten. Speech and the power of speaking leave me. I do not scream, not even as the boy begins to cry, not even when a plate comes down from the back wall with a tremendous crash and splinters into shards that cut my skin in the painless way of razors. Cut too, the boy scuttles away from the broken plate and then his brother hits him again, this time across the back of his tiny head.

That head sinks to pale knees.

The boy pulls him onto his back and carries him out of the house. Temu, the boy explains as he passes me, and dumps him in the shade with his board.

I rush over, I put my hand out.

The boy is already on his feet but turning as if he doesn't know where.

Wait! Ngarima clumps from the bush to herd him away from me, away from the house, using a switch of coconut frond. He stumbles and reaches for her between switchings. She drops her switch and starts to coo, she cups his tiny head in her knife-scarred hands, rubs his cloud of hair, touches his welts and cuts, all the time cooing except when she snaps out an order, catching sight of his slinking-off brother, who doesn't bother to point to the dish broken at the door, or at me.

She holds Temu close.

They stand together for a long time.

After a long time, I follow Ngarima's son into the bush. But follow isn't exactly what I do, I just take his path. I am so confused and full of fear for the small head, the wind-milling arms, the beating, I just walk. I guess I choose the bush because that's the way the boy went who beat him back, who saved me, and if I need saving again he is the one to follow. I don't care about the things in my room any-more—or I forget to care, it is his room anyway. I am the trouble if there is trouble to be pointed at, to be windmilled away.

Ngarima's son is gone from the path by the time I take it. I walk and walk and see no one, no brother or child or man wandering with a machete. I walk and I am pregnant with that child, the boy is flailing his arms around inside me, I am wondering what's wrong? Then the head is too easy coming out, I smile at the wriggling arms until I see the rest and can measure what's wrong against what's right.

My son is about Ngarima's son's age, stalkier though, less woe-eyed but just as fidgety. My son's fidgets are mine. I have to keep going, I have to keep working. Even when he was a baby I worked at this business of illusion, putting con in the game, the game in the con of telling people they must drink things like Paradise in a bottle. I have an imagination that makes that work. But I'd never imagined a child in paradise being wrong.

I'm afraid of people, yes, even children, who aren't right, whose heads are too small or too large or wrong. I suppose I'm more afraid of them when I'm on an island. In another country where you drive past or stare and then turn your head and leave money and move on, I'm not so afraid. It is part of the country, why you are not them.

Now I have his room.

I walk on and on, but I know I can't keep the shore from showing up. I want to avoid it and its lagoon with the tiny head maybe already back in it. Let they who seek out the uneasy bits all islanders bury, seek. I will walk.

I walk until I see a pig in the way, a big pig. I walk to one side of the path and give way to that pig, his bristly back, his huge behind. But his front bears tusks, and he's annoyed, I've annoyed him as he roots with those tusks at a fallen fruit and has to lift his tusked snout just as I am passing on veritable tiptoe past his fruit.

He makes his noise.

I pick up a fruit and hit him in the face with it. He blinks, sniffs it, then crushes it between his jaws, the juice coming through real animal's teeth.

Then he makes his noise again.

I run.

Off the path, everything scratches. I rip my shorts, my legs bleed, my hands tear as I lurch away from the boar into the bush, into the real bush. They may as well tack up boards covered with nails as grow all this stiff stuff so ready for sex that scratches, cuts, jabs, lances what is already dish-shard-sliced.

The bush thickens further with its knife-sharp plants, and I stop. I have to. Besides, the pig's not in pursuit, nor is the windmilling boy. I've gone too far. I have to be lost, though lost on this small island can't be too bad. Maybe lost is good, is just somewhere else. I force myself to smile. I turn as if that's what I want to do.

Where the bush thickens most there's the leftover of a path that veers around it, and I take it more to avoid the plants than for a direction, and at the end of that path is a palm with a wire running up its smooth side, like one plant throttling another. Then I see the house below it.

It is made with fiberboard nailed crookedly to planks and tarpaper and air, but the rusted bolts and barbed wire all around its bottom give it a look of growth, of a succulent's succulent with greening thick walls, of something made fast and abandoned slow.

I look for an opening, a reason for all the bolts and barbed wire, why it's here and not on the beach. Surely the wire's an antenna, surely something inside bounces sound around, if not picture. Inside must be a radio, if not a phone.

I'm free, finding a phone makes me free. The boat is already coming if I can tell it to.

I keep circling.

My ex will send a boat. Although he is the man who forgot me, he is someone who shrinks refrigerators and blows up people for a living, one special effect or another, none of them very special to me after he forgot to pick me up post-delivery, and other better-forgotten events, he could send a boat. But I don't think he thinks of me now.

I hope he doesn't, I hope he's forgotten.

There has to be some place to get in.

It is my son whom I'd call. Miss you, I'd say to him if I could, but it would come out, Brush your teeth. Then I'd make the loud sound of a smack that's supposed to embarrass him, the one that leaves a red butterfly on a cheek.

I stop to think about that butterfly, that call, and then I find the lock.

It's covered with vines and all rusty, a lock I can't knock off with one blow of a machete the way any islander could. I have no machete. I'm probably the only person on the island who doesn't carry a machete.

The shack can't be empty.

Maybe the rust fills in instantly where a sweaty palm turns, or the plants surge over the suddenly bared spot in a single afternoon.

And over what other bared spots on single afternoons? One square mile of island, and how many secrets can such an island harbor?

My shoulders against the door don't so much as flake off rust. I give the door a good kick.

Barclay will open it.

Barclay, I say, let me radio.

Who would look for him in the cemetery? Ghosts, says Ngarima, you don't want to go there. But there he is, drinking, his back up against one of the stones that all lean one way, like recliners, that angle, and hard to see if you are walking by at a clip, which I am, short-cutting and wending and feeling my way back. But I do see.

He gives me his film-star profile, his wet lips settling around a bottle.

Barclay, I say, I've found the shack.

Barclay drinks. The label's imported. What's not imported here?

I squat to his level. At his level, each plot is fenced to the size of a bed and mounded as if there are covers pulled over. In some places the covers are cracked and open. I thought everyone here was afraid of this place, I say. Talk to me, Barclay.

Everyone is afraid, he says. Aren't you? His voice is down deep where darkness sits in a man, where rumble meets those chemicals that make a man or make him weep.

They're not my dead, I say.

No? It doesn't matter, he says. The spirits have blown away anyway. He purses his lips to show me *blow*. All of the spirits.

Quit being so mysterious, I say. It's bad enough you wouldn't take me to the radio.

Radio? says Barclay, sitting up a little. You know, boats used to miss this island even when they started having radar, he says. He drinks again. This is where they always put the inches-to-miles on maps because there is so much blue here they can't resist it, it makes the map look good. He says, Watch the sunset tonight and you will see green fire. Or you used to. He takes another drink. I used to meet women here, he says. No one would bother us.

Barclay, I say, let me radio.

Clare, he says. He says Clare perfectly. The radio doesn't work.

No? I say.

I am a man, and I don't like to say what doesn't work, and I don't like to say it to you, who is not subject to me, but the radio doesn't work. It has no part, the part is gone, I don't know.

He drinks.

You could have told me sooner.

You had your hope.

So when is the boat coming?

It comes when it comes, he says. You should not be so sad.

I like order. Here I can't order up or out, I can't order a thing.

You are a woman.

The inflection sounds kind at first, a little pitying, then it's something I should have thought of, a woman alone with a man.

He offers me his bottle.

Thanks, I say, and I go on with my walk.

Don't mention it, he says after me so that I know it's the mention of the brokenness of the radio that he doesn't want anyone else to hear, not that I shouldn't consider him generous.

I shiver as a mist mists the path in swaths, the way a ghost would, then I run away with an anger that is huge, that cracks.

—·—·—·—·—·—·—·—

I wake in a dream about my son, who is falling, who falls
fast and hard, and I can hear his breath in surprise suck by
the air at my ear, and I run to throw myself to be under
him, a pillow, when someone knocks me down. I writhe to
sit up, to see if my son's all right.

Then I rear back and hit hard.

The part plunging into the air I can't see, this being a
pure night, starless and moonless. I'm not seeing anyway, I
am trying to find a scream where it's made, clutched tight
or asleep, when he and his big hot part get tangled in my
hit and pull down glass, which shatters on the side of the
crate I know is there.

What can I see? I can't see anything.

Get out, you eruption on god's ass, you problem noise
and ghostfucker! That is Barclay, above me. You should
think before you creep so.

Barclay's beating at the curtain that's the front door, its
flowers smoke against the darkness my eyes try to sort. I
stand beside it, wound in more curtain, the sheets here, the
dress here, surely even the slid-off shorts of the man who
stood over me are flowered and red or yellow. I am so

sleepy and shocked I think the red is bleeding into the yellow, or is that because the bleeding should be mine?

Oh well, says Ngarima from her mat, he will be back and try better. Or someone not so clumsy. You see, she says, as I hear Barclay lower himself beside her, they can't break a lamp getting in, they can't fall over things.

It is a custom we should give up for visitors, says Barclay. Let them have the little girls. Look at her, she's not one for them.

Rape, it's called, I say.

It's her fault the lamp is broken, says Ngarima as if I can't hear, rolling over on her stomach beside him.

The boat will bring more glass, says Barclay.

I don't say, Sorry. I don't. I'm having trouble breathing. It must be anger, after that punch. I used the karate of my hand, all that I have, this row of fingers, this bluntness untrained except from the movies, I used it where it hurt, and he tangled his legs together in surprise as he flailed backward and broke the lamp.

I heard him before he broke it, says Ngarima. He was useless, a boy.

They will always try, says Barclay, then he sleeps, drawing the air out of every corner, the loud, sudden snoring like yet another person in the house.

Could Barclay himself be the culprit? I resist crawling between the two of them. I consider fleeing to the shed a few yards away. But there's all that dark between the shed and the house—I could be caught by someone else sneaking up or away. Or is Ngarima's son who sleeps there of an age that slips into houses? Twelve? What do I know? Could it be Harry? I step back behind my curtain.

No guidebook says not to sleep because men make a sport of tupping the tourists. Now only the broken glass protects me. Thank you, Temu, for sparing the one lamp that could break. It certainly wasn't you, you who can't even aim pee without wildness.

I keep my eyes open to the broken glass. No one else, clumsy or not, will tiptoe over it tonight without me hearing his cut cries. Tomorrow I will find the man who did tiptoe by his bloodied feet, the one who fled the room over the lamp pieces, the one who is probably still running over the sharp coral that faces the beach.

Unless he has calluses like all the rest.

Not the sex I expected. I review the few men I've seen here: all smooth-chested adolescents except Barclay and the old men who gamble next to the flagpole at the wharf. Do more men hide in the crevices of this island, lazy ones who don't come down to move copra, who howl with the roosters before dawn and sneak onto women's beds of rice? Men happy about the boat's delay?

I can always use my made-up karate again, and besides, for tonight, the glass will have to do. I keep my eyes wide against the darkness until I have to blink, and blinking, they have to close.

The glass is gone when I wake up. So are the two mountains who sleep but do not guard me just beyond my bed.

Barclay and Ngarima stand under the papaw tree outside, and their voices carry. They are talking about the sex of the tree, whether it will bear anymore, whether by cutting it short it will have better sex. The chicken under the tree pecking at coconut shreds swivels its head between them and their talk, surveying the ground really, moving its lizardy way forward, neck, then ruff, then the machete Barclay carries shakes at the point he is making about tree sex, but he is really aiming, and that is that for the chicken. Suddenly headless, it takes flight, as much as its bush wings allow, it dances and dies, dances and dies, pumping its blood into the sand while the two of them go on arguing.

I don't interrupt.

I break my strong-tourist vow, the one to never complain or whine to another tourist, which would reveal expectation, and all I really want is to be without that, knowing from the ad business how much of that is made up for you anyway, and I break my vow and leave for the guesthouse. Who is surprised about the path I choose? As I choose it, Ngarima waves at me, chicken feathers rising in a white corona around her hand, and Barclay tips his head the way he does when I say, What about a boat wreck?

When Harry comes to his door, he is wearing just a wrap of the flowered sheet around his middle, and what shows above it is where the *Harry* is most appropriate. Since all I have seen him in is what can only be described as planter's wear, I take the wrap as a state of undress and step back in shock. I didn't knock, I say. You're busy, I see, I say.

Knock, he says. But come in. Veelu is about to go.

The woman inside is twisting two coconuts together by their husk-hair. Two heads is what they look like to me, bound in her Valkyrie grasp. I'm all ugly angles next to her, where fat is altogether fine, thin is grim.

She tilts her machete in greeting. Then she lifts her two coconuts and cracks them together so they break open in a single blow.

I smile, and she leaves to skin and dress the coconuts, whatever you do after such a display.

Harry, I say, turning back to him slowly. I give him a sorted-out version of my nocturnal visitor. I end with: I just wanted to know how you were getting along. I try not to say that with female inflection at the end, a question.

I must say the sex is fine, if that's what you're after. He stretches his arms over his head so I see more of his navel. I have at least four women fighting over me.

Oh, good, I say. In turns or at the same time?

As if on cue, another woman shows up, bearing food and wearing Harry's once beautiful shoes as slippers, feet shoved in, untied, with the backs broken.

I'm a happy guy, he says. So you don't like the customs. He walks over to a shirt and trousers splayed across two spiky plants, testing the clothes for dryness, pinching the fabric between his fingers.

I wait. The other woman waits. I hate the tableau feeling I'm getting. A breeze flicks at the ends of the flowered sheet that wraps the woman, shoulders exposed. Sex, sex, sex, laps the lagoon behind her.

He plucks the shirt off the plant and folds it, arm to arm. Well, the boat will take you away soon enough, won't it?

You too, I shrug. Aren't you sorry now you didn't take the last one?

He laughs, his flowered loins straining against the fabric. No, not me. No more boats for me.

I want to swim off Harry and his smug happiness, I want to swim off my own envy—and what? Temu, Barclay—I don't know, maybe it's not wanting to know more, I'm the archetypal tourist. I could swim all the way back to the main island not wanting to know more, I could swim straight through the hot, smooth water past the small black head floating on its board all the way home. Where I do swim is as far as the reef, where the roar of the world starts, and it is there, with the water's violence real and constant, there that I know that I can't swim back, I can't even imagine it.

The ocean, so limitless, such a fence.

Protect yourself, it says. I float on my back. Cumuli pile over me, shadowing the ocean with boat shapes, boats that are always arriving.

I sidestroke my return, trying to slice the water thinner and thinner, my small slashes and wounds from the bush ragged bait for anything that swims under me. Fish muscle through the water in sheaves of color. Why would anyone eat canned fish here? Misplaced mercy, the brilliant stripes fading in the frying pan? That's me, the well-fed one who would change her mind at the first whiff of a fading fillet.

The great silence the fish slice through soothes. I follow a storm of clown fish to an intersection of red and black, where I drift and they rush around, all life and color, into whatever trouble they look for and enjoy. I think *fish* until I am, I dart and swirl and enjoy.

Until I touch sponge. It's a surprise. I retract my feet because what I touch should have been coral, then I push away only to find more sponge, that sponge sponges up an area a hundred feet wide. Dark green, it could look like coral, it could look like just darkness, but as I bounce along, toes sinking, its blind mouthlessness releases a faint gray. It's sponge. I'm probably crushing the foreheads of a million tiny sponges in orgy. I swim away, and in the gray of my going bubbles and sponge corpses rise in suspension behind me, pulse and undulate.

I start swimming to shore, but I'm tired and the shore is so far away and now I'm curious. That was one giant sponge. I dive again to take another look at what I think I've seen, but I look in the wrong direction and all I see are sand squirts, more sand and fish. Or has the giant sponge moved? Or did I make up the soft, porous surface, all that yielding? I dive and gasp again and see nothing, then I swim to shore with all of what strength I have left. Flopping down on the sand, I look out at an ocean that has just shown me what? This ocean that roars and plays so silently.

This ocean that won't talk.

I go to where the men bring their chairs, where I have seen Barclay.

Not many of us sit in the chairs next to the copra shed, midday or not, he says when I ask, Where is everybody? Men leave the island to make money, he says, and the few men there all nod.

It's the same where I'm from, I say, men leave for the city.

Men die without the island, he says.

It's a cash economy, I say. Men die on the island too.

I choose to stay here, he says. He makes his job of greeting visitors, of saying yes, sound very good, makes his place here under the palms on a chair sound great. He is pleased.

What's with the giant sponge? I ask.

Two men stop throwing dice. Giant sponge? Barclay laughs so that others laugh. I have seen those in the movies.

All the men eye me now, my short shorts, my braless sheet-wrapped top.

Which movie? I ask.

She is asking which movie, he says, as if there's an interpreter, as if I am a voice he has thrown. The army's movies, he answers. Let me see, once we saw *The Fly*. Once *King Kong*.

One man pulls his undershirt aside to bare some chest, to beat it.

Nothing's giant around here, says Barclay, turning to me. Everything's small. Small coconuts, small island, small people. Compared to yours.

The army? When was the army here?

Barclay shakes his shoulders as if the question bites at his back. Come here, come here, he says. He tows me over to the flagpole next to the wharf—there's no flag on top, just a bit of metal on the rope hitting the pole—and his audience follows. Did you read our plaque?

It is fastened to the base, I have to squat. *Love makes the world go round*, I read out loud. I thought it commemorated a battle or something.

A battle? An actual smile is what happens across Barclay's face. When we made these houses out of cement, he says, mixing and hauling and spreading, many nights we came to our women exhausted. We did not like that, he says. You see, there's only one thing that grows big around here.

I'm too physical—I step back.

Don't worry, he says when his friends stop laughing. Why did you come, anyway, if you didn't want to be part of our customs? The man who came with you has no problem with our customs. And now it's the water, it's what's in the water. Isn't what's in the water why all people want to come to an island?

I leave Barclay and his dice-throwing friends and find the only shop open among the abandoned and half-built ruins that front the wharf. There I buy a bottle of soy sauce, the condiment of choice for taro, from a young girl who has been sleeping across the counter. The soy-sauce bottle is long-necked and corked—just what I need. But I need it empty, and without thinking to save it for Ngarima or even myself, I pour the contents into pig mash that sits souring in a bucket beside the path. I know it's mash because two pigs fight over it as soon as I leave.

The girl who has sold me the bottle tells me the sauce will fatten the pigs well, so well someone will pay too much for them. Although her hand is very hot when she gives me my change, along with the advice, she smiles all the way across her face.

Children smile with fresh muscles, they don't know where their smiles stop or start. Even in perfidy, they smile so sweetly. I buy a length of suckers from her belt of them and give them out to her and her friends. Except one of the suckers I crack and then wedge down the bottleneck. Then I find matches in my pocket—the Girl Scout in me yet—and the girl lets me buy her last pen so I can write a note on the inside of the matchbook, the perfect-sized paper and tough weight for such writing. Dear Timmy, I print, I miss you and want to kiss you. Here is where I am.

The map I make shows me in the middle, any tourist's rendering. I tear off the cardboard and stuff it into the bottle with the sucker. The children puzzle over the waste of the sweet, licking each other clean of every trace of the suckers' sugar. Except for the smallest, who tucks his little lump-and-stick behind his ear. Then they all talk about what a crook I am to fatten the pig with soy sauce, and I smile wide the way they do.

They follow me to the wharf. I am happy to have them. I want witnesses. After all, if I get a reply I want someone to say I am the one who threw the bottle. But which way to throw it?

I take aim to the west, where the boat disappeared, where continents wait and roads end with cars that sit in driveways with answering machines blinking inside houses. I wind up my pitch to the west with a great series of circles, which sends the kids into screams, then I release the bottle, I throw the bottle as hard as I can into that boat-less, spongy lagoon, throw it off the only jetty on the island, off the pile of coral I was dumped onto when I arrived. After I throw that bottle as far as I can, throw it, a real Little Leaguer mother throw, and it lands with a bright single splash in the middle of the lagoon, it bobs around as if it is getting its bearings, and then, several small swells later, it begins its float back to me.

I pack all the shells I can fit into my bag, wrapping them in underwear and shorts and the one long formal dress I was going to wear at some romantic and thus formal moment, wrapping the shells to keep them from breaking but listening to each one before its interment to hear if the beach inside is the same as the beach outside, to hear if I take their ocean with me.

Just their ocean.

I lay money on the counter over the roach drawer, payment for room and board, all the wasted taro, the too-stinky chunks of tinned mackerel I secretly pushed between the floorboards. I leave my paperback for Ngarima's son, who reads comic books with mold on the pages as bright as the pictures, and maybe Ngarima will like my thongs since she often takes them in the morning before I wake up. I have this wooden fishing spear leaning in a corner, the one Ngarima used to delay me, a seven-foot-long piece of something that surely never grows here and that now no one uses. I'm wondering how to fit it in the airplane that follows the boat: saw it in half?

I do all this at daybreak since I've pretty much given up sleeping after that man-who-broke-the-lamp. *You know which one.* I may be a little too tired from all this not sleeping, but I try not to forget to pack anything, which might happen if the boat loads at dawn as they do in movies to avoid the heat. So I'm in a hurry when I slap my flowered sheet in the air and see bits of my sunburn float off—always the cost of a good tan for me, my souvenir self—and smooth the sheet flat to my rice-bag bed.

I skip breakfast. Seasickness will take care of whatever I manage to get down anyway. I squirrel away a few of those candies I bought from the girl with hot hands for later. How about a note to Harry, wishing him well and thanks for nothing? Instead I write one to Barclay. Your hospitality has been generous. Ba-boom. That's it. What else? Keep that flagpole humming? I write on the back of one of the other island's brochures, and then I prop it up a few inches from Barclay's slack, sleeping mouth.

It's quiet except for the rooster when I step out. The rooster is personally annoyed that I'm up ahead of him and lets me know it. He actually swoops after me in the fraudulent way that fowls have of flying. Or does he just want to crow at another female? As I hurry up the path to the wharf, I pass a pig eating a broken shoelace. It can't be spaghetti. One of Harry's disemboweled shoes? Or is that the end of Harry? The pig grinds down a last delicious morsel.

I smile.

I'm not worried that the wharf is empty, that nobody's piling coconuts or counting out chits as if the boat were imminent. It's such a sleepy place. I poke my head into the tin-roofed shack where they keep the copra, but no one's even asleep inside, and what do I know about how copra's processed? There are coconuts inside.

I take a few steps down the path toward the shop where I bought the soy sauce. It's closed. Then I turn around and put down my bag and walk to the end of the wharf, where I stand and stare. Even with sunlight streaming out over the lagoon in white-hot sheets, even with my hand held over my brow in strict pirate fashion, I can see nothing, no boat past the reef.

I take a seat.

I dangle my legs over the water. I take off my shoes and let my toes slide in. I take out my hat because sun like this will cook me. It's not as if I can't learn. I apply lotion.

Island time, I sigh.

People do come later, a man with a rake, children I don't know who beg for more of my candy—word gets out—a bevy of nameless women who giggle away at something. I ask them all if I'm in the right place and all of them nod, they *yes* me.

I walk back to Barclay's at midday to ask once again if he's heard anything about the boat. As usual, he's not home. Men are not "owned," says Ngarima. I don't know where he goes, she says. She has Temu in a hammerlock and is spooning something green into him that sprays the walls when he sees me.

It's my problem, the boat.

Exiting, I take back my thongs. I'm still angry at Ngarima for how she saw the man in my room as what I had come for, what I needed, what everyone wants. Not that that wasn't what I wanted. But there is swimming and the peace of nowhere and the trinkets of somewhere. Why exactly did she delay me the first time?

I flip-flop all the way around the island, just a quick tour in case a lighter has landed in some unlikely spot I don't know about. No one else is out. The sun is hot: I could be either the mad dog or the Englishman.

I return to the wharf and take up my vigil. I suck candies all afternoon. I give out a few to the children as if the children are a magic that can move events along if they're happy. I don't swim to pass the time. That giant sponge is part of me now, my foot cannot forget the way its swell met me, its size a shiver to be shaken off and pressed out. I am not as haunted by Temu, I'm almost used to his bean head just out of the water. But I'm leaving and taking my pity with me.

Come home, says Ngarima, extending her hand. The sunset's beginning behind her, a deep yellow and red, her hand's color.

_._.._.._.._.._--_ *Part 2*

We call you Vagina Mouth, says the first woman. For those small bites of taro you take. And my name is Spreader. She is Breasts for Three, she is Clam Hold, and Ngarima we call Mouse Touch. You can't guess why.

We are tapping holes into tiny shells. It takes concentration. I have none. I am taking in air like a son of a gun, the names shock me so. More shocking is that they don't laugh. These are their "real" names.

Vagina Mouth! I can't smile now, I can't do anything with my mouth.

I laugh.

The ladies laugh too, finally, but not at my name — at how all my shells fall to the floor when I laugh. We have spent the morning bent over wet rocks, picking these tiny shells off their undersides, and now I have to pick them all off the floor. I wish the little shells would walk away into the cracks the way they do on the rocks so I won't have to, so my bad back won't be part of their talk.

But I like their talk. When laughing women on the way to the beach woke me, I followed them. Ngarima said not to, that in the Bible women together are only trouble. But that's what I need, trouble. You can't live on a missed boat or a book or Barclay's bum radio. You can't stay up all night, watching the door in the rain, or even sit on the wharf day after day as I have done for another week. Besides, Ngarima is full of the Bible since the missionary's visit, or maybe she was full of it before, but I thought that was how they talked here.

Vagina Mouth.

Dresses sewn to the neck the way missionaries like them dry on rocks now bare of all the tiny shells. The women work wrapped in their flowered sheets. For the first time I see the tops of breasts and arms of the island women, pale, thick-muscled protrusions — and the necklaces.

Not the necklaces of shell, which they are putting over their heads as quickly as they are strung, but the necklaces that these necklaces hide, a stitching of scar where the shells lie, a scar so neatly stitched around each woman's neck that I wonder if they're born with it. But surely they die without it, whatever's been taken out having grown huge with the dull sex of multiplication. I have never seen someone with that kind of scar, those operated-on necks. I ask one about the stitching with my eyes and touch my own neck, but the woman won't say, she is singing, they are now all singing and dancing.

The tin roof of the shed rumbles with their singing. I think they pick the shed because it makes singing sound louder. I can't get the words, they sing so many parts it could be a hymn — but it's definitely sexy. The women un-dulate in their seats, they jump up and hula with each other, hip to hip, hip to crotch. Their flowered cloths threaten to fly open with the swaying, their wild undulations. How many are old? Not one. How many ugly? None.

It beats being depressed or boat-nuts. Why have I stuck with Ngarima for so long? Fear of the natives? Of knowing their names? As soon as I know their names, I know too much, I'm accepting the fact of my becoming a castaway.

Now I really know too much, I know their nicknames.

They are poking holes in the shells again, stringing and poking and murmuring the tails of song back and forth, as if they are still singing, as if they never stopped talking. I don't, in my life of phone chat and cocktail talk, often experience women as a whole, as beings together. Now my hands move as slowly as the women's, my hands are not fidgety, trying to leave the island on their own. I make each tap on a shell deliberate, not done to be done. Not even sitting on the porch with Ngarima is being together like this, not even opening her tins of fish, peeling her taro, lighting her stove for food. Barclay must make the difference, the deference to his authority. Instead of asking about the necklaces, I ask, Why doesn't Ngarima come with you?

The ladies smile, the ladies ply their nylon line through the shells. Ngarima, says Breasts for Three, you are not the one for her. The others say I should come to their houses, they will feed me, they will show me.

And besides, says Spreader, her son isn't with the others. The ladies cluck.

You mean the one with the small head? I ask.

They laugh at me, they toss up their hands as if he hardly counts. It's the other. He won't seduce the girls, says Breasts for Three. All the other boys go off with girls except for him. Except for that other boy and one more, says another. Some other boys who don't like girls.

One fewer hiding for me in the night, I decide. Does he like boys? I ask.

I have crossed a line. They gasp their shock, but I see some hide smiles, so I know that their shock is for me, not for them. He is not that, they say, straight-faced. Oh, no. He doesn't sleep with the girls because he is working.

I have to laugh. I don't want to because it's not right to laugh at what others believe, but I do. A twelve-year-old boy scorned because he's working instead of putting in time with the girls? I have to laugh, and they laugh too, but it's not the same laugh, it's an uneasy, pro forma, what-will-she-do-next? laugh.

The laugh is interrupted by a cry.

The cry comes closer, and the women quiet, they stop their laughing and their plying of line. They look at each other.

It's just a baby, I say.

A young girl, the one men paint when they paint islands, wanders in with the crying bundle. She sits on the ground beside us, she tries to quiet it. Her breasts, hard against a band of flowered cloth, are two dark stains of seeped milk, dark as her eyes that say *tired* and *faraway* together when she lifts them once, trying to loosen that band, trying to get the women to help her loosen it and quiet the baby.

Breasts for Three and two others surround her, they talk low to her about holy water and the missionary and what he told her, then they take the baby away, very slowly, as if the baby will stop crying just by their gentleness. They tell her everything will be fine, and one of them lays the baby in a nest of palms outside the shed while they talk to her, while they tighten the band around her. The young girl begins crying now like the baby, so quietly, while the women stroke her hair and murmur about the baby and the young girl and about how she must leave it.

I walk across the shell-strewn floor, each step crushing more shells that are crawling off.

The baby's still crying, so low it could be two boughs of trees that don't grow here crossing each other in a cold wind. Why let it cry? I'm about to lift up the bundle when I have to feel around it to get a grip, and this grip-getting pulls back its blanket, and despite the dazzling sun after the dark shed, I see its one eye. Where the other should be is skin. A sort of skin. But pulling back the blanket that much frees it, lets all the baby out. It rolls free, it shakes to a stop on the ground like jelly, and you can see it has no anus, you can see too why the jelly—it has no bones.

I turn my head as if that will block what I've seen, then I get up out of my crouch over the baby. It's still making its noise. I fling the blanket over it, then I try to put it back together, jelly, eye, and all.

Clam Hold takes it away from me.

It's almost dark, dusky enough so that a single gull overhead looks pink from below, when I find Ngarima's son. I've been walking in circles to get land to continue under my feet as if it will lead somewhere. As if by walking I could get there, get to where the boat must be. I walk to be nowhere, and there is Ngarima's son, with two friends. Each of them is digging into driftwood with a sort of hoe just the way I have seen people do it on film, and they are digging with these hoes to make a hole wider just as I come crashing through the bush.

I thought you said there were no boats here, I say as I come right up to them and their boat through the dark.

Tupaka, they all screech, and run off together.

I am reaching behind with both my arms, holding my arms backward, fingering the keys. Or what would be keys if a piano stood in Harry's shack. I am humming all the parts to a melody I once liked, ghostly and grand, that I know will impress. I always impress when I play the piano backward, humming or singing. Though less in parlors than in bars — so few parlors with pianos, so few pianos unless they're in bars.

I am thankful for Harry. Harry knows the tune, he even knows the score, he knows this is a piano I am gesturing toward, he can see I can finger. Without a piano, no one can say you missed a note or you play without feeling, mechanically, like a parlor trick. Anyone else on this island without parlors would want to lock me up for the strangeness of it — or laugh. People laugh at the strange first. But maybe not at jelly babies. Even Harry did not laugh at that. But perhaps Harry would have laughed at my playing the piano if I had not told him what I was doing. Perhaps the others would understand if I told them about it first, pianos being the missionary's power band, the thumping equivalent of salvation earned, those gold chords. Perhaps old ivory from a missionary's piano could be dug up, an F sharp sticking up out of the coral, with the car parts.

Harry has plied me with drinks, and that is how I begin to play. "To ply" suggests that I am pliable. I play. He empties the last of a bottle of scotch into a pitcher—no, a cracked coconut half, all he ever drinks from. He's scraggly-bearded now, and all around him lie playing cards from tricks and games he's tried to teach his ladies, but they won't play, he says, they want only one thing. That one thing, I repeat, but my piano playing drowns me out, I am drowned.

It is time for him to tell his story. He can tell his story if he wants. But he doesn't have to explain what he's doing here if he doesn't want to. Instead, he tells about being in Afghanistan as a hippie. It was a long time ago, he says, and I believe him. His hair was that long, he says, he says he had plenty of it then. It hung in clumps, the blue and pink dust of the cliffs that they passed clumped it, with the grease that was part of having that hair.

Why am I telling you this? he asks.

You said you don't like things hanging. I point with my pinkie at the twist of straw and feather dangling over us. Someone hung it there, the Valkyrie, who is away, who is coming back any minute, who is gone just for now.

Oh, yes, he says. Veelu is afraid of the *tupaka*. You know, ghosts? This is supposed to catch them.

I touch my hair the way a woman does who was born brunette, who remembers she's blond. Ghost. I start playing something soft with long, tiddly fingers, something that would scare boys in the bush.

She was hung, the woman I was with, he says.

Good grief. I stop playing and sip at the scotch from the coconut's rim. Hung how?

She drove the truck. I was a hitchhiker, her hippie. She was going somewhere she was told to, and she was sad because in the same mail as the assignment the man she wanted wrote that he wanted someone else. She drove the truck fast through all that pink and blue, she was a cloud with wheels when she picked me up. We camped when she came to a stop and a cloud of blue and pink settled in our hair, our teeth, and our necks. We zipped our bags together, we wormed our way over the cinders of the fire I built from blown-around bushes, burning the bags a little, and we laughed about it, about that kind of love. That was the only time I heard her laugh.

I am looking out his window, where the moonlight is too bright. I want to interrupt, but I can't get the words arranged. He stops talking, and what am I supposed to say? I sip and watch the shadows that the twist of straw and feathers make against the moon.

She could drive fast over those rutted, washed-out tracks. She drove as if she could drive out the bad letter she carried, as if driving away drove him away. She drove hard into a herd of goats. Goats were always on or off the road. She drove in and hit one. Or so she thought. The dust of the goats, the dust of her truck slowed down—who could tell?

When she saw what it was, she was out of the car. When they bore him away, she followed them. I followed her. I wasn't going to sit in the truck and wait around. I wasn't going to drive away with her truck either, though I did later. What I remember most about following is the women who rose up out of the big clumps of dirt and wailed over the boy. The blue and pink walls of the cliffs wailed.

We waited a day. It was decent of us, decent of them to bring us food, they who unrolled mats and let us lie in a warm room all night, lie without sleeping. The room had a hole in the roof that children and birds passed over. Only those who brought food came down the ladder that was left for us against that hole. I used it only once in the night, to pee off the roof.

She didn't talk about how much she loved that man that night, she didn't even talk about the boy, who he could have been. I didn't make hippie talk. I showed her my flute. Did you have a flute in those days or just a piano?

I had a flute.

Well, then, you know how I could try to sound Afghani with my flute there in the dark. But I also did "Yankee Doodle," "Hi-Ho Silver." She wanted me to play anything. I didn't know her, she was an older woman with a man who didn't want her and a job waiting for her at the end of her drive. She dug latrines because she was a woman. That was what women did then, you know, to be women, to show they could be men if they wanted. She was helping the people, and she had another job at the end of the drive to show she could help, though she hadn't been helping long — she knew about as much of their language as I did. After I put down the flute, I smoked what I had — she was asleep by then — and listened to the wailing.

We climbed out in the morning. Goats were swarming all over the place, as noisy and jammed up as they had been the day before on the road. But now no one was straightening them out. More people than lived in these places had come to wail, men to one side of a clearing, wailing women on the other. The boy was carried between them on a litter, wrapped tightly in blue and pink cloth. You could believe cocoons made butterflies, I remember thinking then.

I wasn't so stoned that I couldn't get the ladder out of the hole and over the side of the wall. She made a big deal out of helping me and almost fell off. The men met us at the bottom. They were all weeping now, not wailing—I had never seen so many men crying before. One of them put out his hand and she took it.

That was dumb, I say.

She said, It is raining, and pointed at their eyes full of tears, and they smiled. She lived with them, or with people like them where she came from. I don't think it was dumb.

So they hung her?

He doesn't look up at the plaiting that hangs from the ceiling, the only thing hanging, the thing that makes shadows out of the moonlight that plays here.

They ignored me. I waited around for her to come back, but she didn't, so I walked back to the truck, thinking I would drive it over, pick her up, and get going, but once I swung myself up into the driver's seat—there was still blood on the windshield—I realized she had the keys. I had to walk back to the village, over all that humped earth that the women seemed to come out of the day before.

And yes, there she was. I was so set on the keys in her pockets in that weird way you get when you are stoned that I remember panicking because she was nude, not because she was dead. Then I tried to run away. Nobody would let me. Not even the goats that came swirling around the first corner of my running. Who can get away in the middle of a bunch of goats? But it turned out that all they wanted was to give me the body. They didn't want a body that wasn't theirs, they didn't want to bury a body that had buried one of theirs. It was up to me to cut her down, to wrap her in her clothes—her arms and legs already were no good to move—and carry her now wood-heavy body over all those dirt clods back to the truck and drive her away.

And the moral of the story?

He looks around. Is someone listening? He says, Don't think you can help.

I can't help. I wasn't even thinking of helping. I'm angry I missed the boat. I just want to get out of here.

I keep watch on my hands. He is very attractive now, without his women, with all this scotch and his story.

He stretches way up and takes down the hanging, plaited pandanus.

We're not really here for them anyway, I say. We're here just to eat and sleep, I guess, but not for them. We're in the way for them.

He drinks the rest of what's in the coconut.

You know, it's not the secret of life that people always want, he says. That's easy, that's a man and a woman, we can even do that with test tubes. It's the secret of death. What happens after life isn't too interesting. So what if you could live death, wouldn't that get you a little closer?

You are guessing now, I say. What am I not seeing? I once heard a hairdresser ask, and I felt fear. It's not funny.

You know what else about this island? he says when he stops laughing. The most famous story about this island?

Listen, the ticket agent didn't even spell this place right, let alone tell me about it. I came because the main island was a bore, because the crew for a drink called Paradise got tired of me playing the piano backward at night, because all I could get in the seashells was car roar and not waves.

You want another story?

I like you, I say.

You wouldn't look at me someplace else.

This is an island, after all, I say. Tell me the story, I say. You have to keep inventing or else the island closes in, goes cold with too much truth.

He looks out his window. The first white woman to set foot on this island was the mistress of a Captain Goodenough, who wasn't quite good enough, and so he left her—in payment of a debt. Or in a hurry? Who knows? Or had he just had enough of her and wanted to exchange her for an island woman? Or did she give him syphilis and he knew it?

She liked the place, she wanted to stay.

Whatever. Anyway, she got herself in trouble immediately. Whoever couldn't have her fought with the rest until they realized nobody was having her. They decided to solve the problem most democratically — by eating her. A little of her for everyone.

Sex and food, men are always getting them confused. So, what about it? Are you trying to warn me? I'm the dainty little dish set before the king?

I'm not a bit drowsy now.

Don't think you can help, he says, and he pushes me toward the door.

Hey, I don't know any more about you, I say.

You'll think of something. He frowns, patting his chest where a cigarette might be.

Aha — an addict? I say. I know you better already.

Oh, no, not me. He grimaces.

Veelu waits outside. She can't look in, there are no windows except toward the water. She can only listen. I walk past her with the swagger of someone who knows more than she, of someone who has heard his stories and understands what he means.

Later, I'm sorry.

This week I will stay in the water up to my neck until the boat comes, and in the meantime the island will wash off and I will have nothing to fear. Besides, I will drink and eat nothing, especially not drink. I will be safe.

I am sane. I am sane. This is the sane thing to do.

I slump into the water, just letting my nose and mouth stick out, but I'm so white, white-faced and white-headed, that I can't be a rock or a seal or a post. I wish for Harry and his whiteness beside me, a hundred Harrys dimpling the lagoon so I can't be picked out by color, so I can't be picked out. Oh, if I have to be here, let me be fitted with the parentheses of a tourist, the ones that let you not be where you are and not be at home at the same time, the ones that are safe.

Ngarima says a stupid girl can't stay in the water all the time like a dog with bugs. You'll get sick and we'll be blamed, she says. She asks how I am.

Fine, I say. Just in for a morning dip, I say.

Ngarima has been slapping what I think is rope against a rock. She watches me.

Who's more interesting than me? Here, when I open my mouth, everyone else shuts theirs. Here, when I say I'm going nuts, nobody says anything until two hours later, when someone asks, Is this where the nuts are?

I am not facing Ngarima. I am answering her with my face to the sea, as if I should not take my eyes off it, as if a boat will pass by if I do. If only I could climb to the top of the tallest coconut and keep watch and stay in the water at the same time. What was screaming this morning? I ask, half submerged.

A pig. Pigs don't like to die.

I clear my head from the water. Just a pig. Good, I say.

It was the pig you gave your bottle of soy to, that fat one.

That one? Oh, yes, right. I did buy a bottle of soy sauce. I shut my mouth. That pig was happy with that soy sauce. What about its bottle? I arch my neck over the water to see if it's still afloat. Things do float against the morning brightness—is that a bottle? Or Temu?

I can't tell.

We are having a celebration, she goes on. For you, she says. And for the other one, Harry. We haven't had visitors for such a long time that we are making a party to show our respect. But for such a party, we have to wait for the sauce to sour, for one of the pigs to get big.

Ngarima, I say. I am stopped from saying what a fine thing this is to do, but unnecessary, how many pigs do you have? let alone how ungrateful I am to be here where pigs scream first thing in the morning and deformed babies roll

out of mats and giant sponges lurk, and what's wrong with
Temu anyway? when I see what's coiled on her shoulder.
Intestines, garden-hose long. They are all clean, I see that,
flat and clean, there's a bottle of Joy in her hand, I see its
bubbles not far away, a little extra foam, and a little something brown swirling around me in the water.

So much for the water.

I get out and shake myself dry.

Another pig is dying behind us. Why not a woman? The
scream is high-pitched enough, furious and animal
enough. A woman in high heels, a hoofed woman. The lagoon goes red, and deep inside it starts glowing, it starts to
scream itself.

A boat is coming, isn't it? I say. In time for leftovers?

Ngarima starts. A boat will come, she says. Yes, she
says. Her *yes* sounds like *yes*, it is possible a boat will come
like the sun will rise, the day end.

Behind us men throw dice against the church wall, the
noise of their play followed by soft ha-ha's that could be
laughter or something else I don't understand. One of
them flicks on a cordless razor. It has to be cordless—there
are no plugs. Then he brings that buzzing razor over to the
dead pig and begins to shave it.

When was the army here last? I ask.

The army doesn't come here, Ngarima says She is
watching the surf the way I do, but the way she watches is
better—she can see past it, she can see into it.

But Barclay says it comes. He told me they showed
movies.

She squeezes her hose again. Yes, a sort of army still comes. She gives me a look that I equate with their present tense: every word she says revealed to her as she says it.

Over the sound of pig death begin the quick strokes of a drum. They are a heartbeat's, doubled. Ngarima's son walks down the beach from where that sound is coming to take the hose from Ngarima.

Go practice the dance, she says to me. Until it's time.

I look out at the empty ocean. The dancing faces it.

In second grade we had to dance, I say to Ngarima's son. We put on skirts made of paper cut into wavy lengths that stained, and we had to wriggle. I wriggled hard the way a robot would so no one would laugh. I hated it when they laughed.

Ngarima's son is already smiling.

I follow him to where four women weave something about birds with their hands over their hips, and their hips say something else in circles, each hip saying it exactly the same way as the next woman's. Only the size of the hips varies, and as fast as I see this, the size doesn't matter, one matches the other in what they say with how they move. It's not that collecting-shells kind of dancing, that bursting forth, but the engine of the island in serious precision. Maybe this is Morris dancing, maybe this is square dancing, but when the men waggle their knees open and shut and dance close and dance closer to the women's hips, it isn't folk, I can't dance it with my parents paying for the outfit.

Ngarima's son dances, boy enough to make a farce of the dance and its peacock engagement, and the other men are old, the other end of what wags. But they wag, they shimmy and wriggle up to me, scissoring their knees and legs while the drum tats louder and harder and I start to sway.

You have to put your arms up to sway right. The hips need room. But with your arms up, men find places to hold on to, the curve and the bulge where the breasts grow, though they don't touch me. But then I don't sway much.

At a nightclub on the island where we shot Paradise, all the tourists were asked to dance. I either kept to the back or else I did it, with my face flushed and watching the back the way a ballerina would, to keep from falling into their precise swaying that pressed toward me again and again without touching. Touching is never the point. Everyone who is not an islander is a Methodist when it comes to this not-touching dance, we have no limbs that correspond to theirs, all we can do is touch and not sway that well.

I try not to breathe, I try not to let any of the island into me. I just dance and forget that I am here by being so here. I say nothing to anyone, even when they shout *Vagina Mouth* and clap out my path.

I am saying no to their beer that they make out of what? when Harry comes and says, Don't be stupid. Hearing that so soon a second time makes me think I might be. If a boat comes this time, even they will miss it is what he says when it's almost dark and doesn't matter.

I think of my son. This island I'm on is a planet drifting farther and farther away. Not drifting the way planets do on film but screeching along at a pace, that second per second they calculate that wrenches us away from the other stars and wandering planets. My son is standing on a street corner on another faraway planet—just like one of those classroom models—and he's waiting for the traffic to part so he can run across and somehow join me, but the traffic is part of the orbiting too, it's the ocean, and the street corner I'm on drifts farther and farther away.

We are all soon slick with scented lagoon water and flower-crowned with stiff white fragrant ginger. We each take a seat in front of half a cold chicken and three pounds of pork and blood pudding and coconut pudding and bananas for garnish on banana leaves and a half coconut shell filled with sauce four weeks soured. Barclay and many others make speeches, long, formulaic speeches that I smile through, smile as if my life depended on it, which perhaps it does, *they* now being *us* to me, us with our Vagina Mouth talk, with our sickness and secrets, with all this air I breathe, the food we will eat together—yes, I will, I smell the food, even the dead pig's dark blood in pudding makes my stomach fierce, I will eat and meet them, stomach to stomach, as if in dance, and when they speak so long and full of flattery, I decide they are going to ask me to do something for them.

But they ask nothing. Or nothing I understand.

I dance and dance, and even Harry dances with me
once. He is as stiff as wood, despite all the beer they ladle
out for him with their oil cans. But I am Vagina Mouth,
who cares what I do? They shout when I swivel, they roar
when I bump him with my hip. Harry doesn't care, Harry
drinks enough beer to dance his stiffness wild with all the
island women, from crone to toddler. The men egg him on,
they shove their fists into the air when the drumming gets
going, they thrust themselves forward at the torso, they
yell in their language, Get it on, the way men's language
does.

If I should not eat the food or drink the water, the beer
must be worse—that is what beer is for. I get loaded, I
wander away into the dark. The path I take turns past
where coffee tins are planted with whatever's growing
right beside them, and beer bottles surround a chair in the
center of that tin garden, so many beer bottles they could
be a collection, or an offering. Behind this leans a house
with a defeated roof, and the house is dark and doorless,
and what wafts out in the heavy, humid darkness is the

smell of suppuration, of scabs picked and reopened, and what sound accompanies it is as constant as a series of waves. It's not the weepy, wet sound I hear from Temu that carries over the water and makes Ngarima rise but guttural and fresh like a hose tightening around someone, some peculiar sound that realizes itself, like constant pain, in the present.

I am not curious. I don't want to see who or how. The pain is the island's, the pain is only a matter of time.

— ·— ·— ·—

It is the next day. The next day I have my hangover, and it is one you want to climb out of and leave the head behind, the head so not your own it is surely borrowed and overdue, thank you very much, but what I see in my head is three perfectly can-shaped cylinders of corned beef and a side of immaculately white rice — Barclay's party food from yesterday. That's what sticks in my mind. He did not eat the chicken and pork and banana and boiled blood squeezed onto the banana leaf, he did not drink from a single coconut.

I have never seen him drink from a coconut. From none of the coconuts he opens for me, three a day, not from any of those has he taken even a single sip.

I sit on the porch wearing a taro-leaf poultice and between throbs I think. Barclay sits on the porch too, for once here, and without a poultice. But he is slow today, very slow, and as soon as he sits he falls asleep and soon begins to snore his thunder snores. Someone else will have to tell me, someone else will say why they don't object or make fun of him and his corned beef and rice and no coconuts. I hold my poultice to my forehead and use the fingertips of my free hand to ease myself up to standing without disturbing too much of the pounding. I make for the two steps off the porch to ask Ngarima, who is rooting in the bush.

But there, just over the edge, under the flowering plant that a stick I dropped turned into, lies a small overturned box. It kills me to bend over to pick it up, my poultice slips, blood rushes into my heavy temples, but the glimpse I have is of photos inside. Beside it lies the ripped spine of an album that looks like just a curl of bark if you are sitting on the porch.

A boy I've never seen on the bow of a ship with Barclay. That's the first picture.

The others show less, the boy at the bottom of a set of steps, the same boy in a bed looking bad, pink flesh under brown, Barclay beside a gravestone with what looks like Minnesota behind it, grass and trees whose leaves fall and a power line and a station wagon.

My hands begin to shake.

Bravo, says Barclay behind me.

Bravo? I repeat. He doesn't say it like *congratulations*.

He takes the photos from me. Temu, he shouts.

The army's Bravo, it was their big test here, he says. He is speaking without looking at the photos, he speaks with his eyes shut, he speaks from an old pain in his head. Or really the test was over there, he says. He points one hand into the wind without looking at it. But then the trades blew and brought the test here, and after a while my son is taken away with me on this boat to your country, and I go home later alone.

You know too much, I say, holding my hands so they don't shake so. That's why you don't eat.

He takes the broken album back from me.

Temu! he calls out. Temu!

Temu doesn't come dripping up out of the lagoon.

Barclay sits and smooths the photos, puts them back into the box with the others. He is still smoothing when Temu shows up, not dripping. One of Temu's hands clutches more photos so tightly that surely they can't be flattened back into the box. The other hand flexes as if he's ready for more.

Instead of beating him, Barclay pulls him close. Temu starts to moan, to roll his eyes, tries to hit his small head against the wall behind them.

I am them, and I am we.

— ·— ·— ·—

Bravo is just what he says it is, says Harry.

It sounds Italian, I say. An Italian perfume.

Ha, says Harry. It sounds self-congratulatory, something real American.

I look out his window. The sun bloodies itself going down.

You knew all about this before you came?

Harry sits on his floor, touching one of the many pink, slick shells that line one wall. A few roaches crawl out of one of them, but that's where the roaches live — everywhere.

I'm starting over, he says. That's all. No one will follow me here.

I nod. It's quiet for a while.

You have a son, he says. You talk about him.

I walk around the room. School, you know. Sports. I never know what he is thinking unless he wants something. I'm the one with custody.

Custody, I say again. What a weird term.

Possession's nine-tenths of the law, he says. You think you possess him.

You never possess anybody, that much I know, I say.

Sure, he says. That's what you think. He works his finger into the crenellated folds of one of the shells. The island's a possession, what kind of owning is that?

He starts talking about half lives, how the cells repair so fast they overrepair, how they actually have a life and a half. He stops talking.

You're afraid, aren't you?

You're the one who's afraid, he says. You're the one coming to me.

I'm no volunteer. I squat by the shells. You had a life once, you were married too, I'll bet.

So what? he says.

You're a criminal, aren't you? I ask.

I could be a saint, he says. I could be Bogart. Vagina Mouth, he says.

At least I have a name, at least they're not cooking me in the *umu*.

The way we cooked them? he says.

I have to get off this island, I say.

I stand and look out again.

He is not listening, standing beside me the way you do when you're looking inside instead of out.

Ngarima's son is the bright one. I have to change the subject, there's only one subject. There's always one bright one.

He picks up another shell. If you were a little brighter and learned a little of their language, you'd see who was bright.

Quit it, I say after my moment of shame. Did you push drugs or was it money you lost for someone in the stock market?

Maybe I'm an artist, he says. The island is very beautiful, isn't that what most people say?

He turns away and rotates the shell by its scrolls, a rotation that makes me dizzy because I watch it instead of him in our silence, and then our silence changes, it's the way talk stops on pillows, how lust is drawn out and out and you can't see it until it's right there.

I walk over and kiss him then, with his finger caught between the lips of a shell, before he can say anything else. I am reckless in a sad way, with the ghost catcher back up and swaying, the windows open, the not quite pitch dark.

We arouse each other, and I get it. This is how you escape here, you don't swim or drink or lie in the sun. You just do this. As advertised. As appropriate. And why not? All the rest of the world has its *why nots*, its *don'ts*, its best

ways to make the world blank out, the four-letter word
work, work, work—somewhere it must be something else,
this.

Good, says Harry when I tell him this, even though it is
plain he knows it, has not struggled against the cliché-in-
your-face. I hold him and escape, but I do not forget that
surely one of his women waits not far away. Then he pools
coconut oil in my navel and spreads it with his whole body,
and I do forget.

I do not want a child with no bones is what I tell him.
No bones, no bones. I don't say *disease* or even *unwanted* the
way the rest of the world does. He drops rocks into his
condoms so they will sink in the lagoon and play anemone
with the sea squirts. He fishes out the rest of his packets
from his snakebite kit and gives them all to me—I am the
only one here who can have this fear. We lie together,
hands on each other.

The bushes shake.

I sit up fast, I lean into the dark.

Harry presses his face against his screen, and the
rustling stops. He stands up, a bear in moonlight. Who's
that?

Whoever's outside doesn't answer, but the rustling picks
up. We both look into what light stripes the beach, the
edge of the bush where Harry likes to hang his wash.

Between the dark angles of Harry's newly cut-off suit
pants, between his now faintly gray white shirt and a dangling of suspenders, stands no jealous woman hefting her
machete. Instead Ngarima's son and his two friends drag

their boat down to the beach. It's what they work on at night instead of girls, I whisper to Harry. He laughs and strokes my back around to my nipple and kisses me.

We stop and watch them launch the boat with curses and squeals. They shove and they pull, and the boat sits so low in the water I'm sure that when they scramble in it will fill and sink. But they heave over a coil of rope and then something else, and then they fit themselves in, the three of them, and hoist a sail. Then they paddle to the edge of the lagoon, paddle hard, singing softly while they shoot forward in rhythm, then they wait at the reef's mouth, then they shoot through the reef and disappear.

Hey, says Harry, my clothes are gone.

His suspenders still dangle, but the rest of the bush is bare.

Harry looks all around his shack, but there's nothing else. All I have left are the legs from the cutoffs, he says.

I'm more woebegone. Harry, I say. You know what just happened?

All my clothes were stolen, he says.

These kids aren't coming back, I say. They're gone, they're out of here, they've escaped.

We stare at the reef, its foam sealing their exit. Where are the right stars? that boy asked me a couple of times, says Harry. I didn't know.

How long do you think it took them to make that boat? I ask. How long would it take? I ask.

A year, maybe, Harry whispers.

— · — · — · — · — · — · — · —

The dark is all that's left then. We do what we can in all that dark and disappointment, then we dream. But what I dream is no dream: flying fish did rise over our ship, and a woman did catch one over the lifeboat I slept in, she did slice it open and offer me its still thrashing body, and I did look down at its entrails shining and sinking in the moonlight and say, Yes, please. And the raw fish tasted milky the way men do.

It is too easy: the quaking body, the salty air. I am uneasy. I thrash and wake up with tears on my face. I don't wake Harry when I have enough light to go. Instead I look for my thongs.

I'm at Barclay's doorstep when I find them. Thongs have a life of their own here, someone is always taking them, so they show up before you do. Is this someone reporting my night out with Harry? I am still working my feet into the thongs when the first long wail catches me. It's not a pig this time, this time it is a woman. A woman wails. There's no other sound like it, it's female. And there, at the flowered door pulled back, stands Ngarima, wailing. For what? My one night's absence? Nothing I could do could produce that sound from someone. That sound frightens me. I don't move, I don't move or go forward.

Breasts for Three stands beside Ngarima now, and she wails as well. She is holding the moldy comic book that Ngarima's son kept hidden in a basket in the cookhouse and a broken thong that he'd repaired with tape. Then another woman crowds the doorway behind them. Her wail joins theirs, their three bodies go taut with the grief of wailing.

I stand there. It's not about me.

Barclay comes around the back of the house. He is rigid, walking forward, holding Temu by the neck, pushing Temu and his windmilling arms around me and the women and into the house without a word to any of us. Barclay is crying.

I sit in the shade in front of Barclay's place. All day people bring candy wrappers, bits of twine, a tiny toy, a stone, whatever Ngarima's son touched or liked, a sprouted coconut with Styrofoam insides that Ngarima eats on the porch, salts with her tears. Once a woman comes who wails louder than Ngarima, carrying a yowling cat. She is the mother of one of the other boys I saw with Ngarima's son, and it is his cat she carries, that claws at her arm. The mother of the third boy arrives, bringing only a pair of the boy's shorts.

Boys do this, Breasts for Three tells me when she has no breath left. Boys get restless, they build a boat, and then they must use it. How to stop them? Then they get lost. They don't know how to go—we don't know anymore ourselves. Sometimes later someone will see them in Singapore or Cairns, but they will not be boys then, they will be the ghosts of boys having gone so far in these boats. But never mind—most boys die.

At sea? I don't say.

I also don't say I saw him, I could have stopped him. I say, Maybe they are only trying the boat out.

Breasts for Three says they chose to launch the boat at Harry's because there no one would see them. We see nothing, she says. I have to agree, I have to nod and look away. She says everyone else knew what the boys were doing, but no one can keep a boy even if he has no money for a fare. Boys like leaving. No one else wants to leave, this is our home—paradise. Only if someone needs medicine do they leave.

It is dark when I decide to slip inside and gather whatever of my things Temu hasn't gutted or strewn, and I shove all of it under my bag of rice. Barclay holds the boy's arms back by the elbows when I lift my curtain to go back out. Barclay holds him, but Temu struggles to free himself. He wants to what? Take his grief out on me? Does he have grief? Or does he want to beat me for just being there?

I will go sleep on the beach. Sleeping on the beach is what you're supposed to do on a perfect island like this anyway, I don't know why I haven't done it sooner. Temu certainly wanted me out, even if he does sleep elsewhere, even if Ngarima says I must sleep in his room. Anyway, if the beach is hot, so are the beds. I shake the hands of each of the chief mourners slumped in wailing stupor on the porch, and I touch many of the hands of all the others who have come, who weep too, even the men, whose weeping frightens me, who wail men-wails and beat on the coral and each other, then I go to pick out a stretch of beach that will do for the night, and damn the roving rapists, the dying half lives.

Mosquitoes graze in every depression, they come out of the bush as another sharp, cutting part of the bush, a part that flies. Where two palms grow close, where the wind presses these palms flat the way it is always blowing, where the wind picks up sand in sheets and stings so no mosquito stays, a place not far from where the car parts rust in their coral colors, not far from where a boat might come if it came, I hollow out a place anyway and line it with my flowered cloth. I don't dig too deep, not to China, not to whatever's left of a jelly baby. Then I lie down to test my hollow for later, pull palm fronds and scrap leaves over me, and I fall asleep, my sleep with Harry having been slight.

Real night is about to fall when I wake. Loud singing wakes me, from people who don't see me, filing past, singing with all the lust taken out, with no fists thrust up into the sky, no hips swinging and rolling. They file past my place, and they carry things — the comic book, the thong, the toys — and two men, Barclay one of them, and one woman walk out past the wharf into the lagoon with these things that they weight with stones and make into parcels, that they drop in.

The boys are gone, they are buried.

Returning, Barclay passes me, Ngarima passes. I'm now standing beside a line of moving people, trying to look as if I know what it is that they feel. *There's nothing you can say* is what I would say to excuse myself, but that wouldn't be nothing enough.

I move to the wharf after they've all gone. I expect to see the bright newsprint of the boy's comic book floating back in minutes, the way my bottle did, but nothing shows. A few things do get away. Then a star falls out of the sky, and I know as I watch the bright night with all the strange constellations built into its darkness that even the sky gets away.

My son got away.

He is dead. Dead for a year—a year, is it? Dead for however long it takes to work that hard after. An accident is that hard. An accident is nobody's fault, you're on your own, there's just a doctor to sign papers, your ex to tell you how stupid you were to let it happen. That's why there's no telling anyone, there's no mourning—I am that stupid.

He is not dead. See the stars, see the rain that fell, the ocean?

I get back down into my pit, and I weep at last.

Morning.

Why not walk to where the middle of the island might be, where fewer people walk and where I can't see the ocean over either shoulder?

Why not *not* walk? I stop anywhere, I look into the bush that has bitten me—or is that mosquitoes? I look into it, but there's no picture made in my head of bush or bugs.

I find myself sitting. I find myself making earplugs from the soft centers of flowers, then I curl on my side away from ants and mosquitoes and bush and I shut my eyes. I dream about nothing, I dream about living on a beautiful tropical island that I have made out of nothing, as advertised.

Flowers rain down. I can't sleep anyway. I can just breathe in and out, I can just keep my eyes closed and dream. I sit up. I brush the flowers off with the dream, but they release their smell, the one sense I can't block. I rub their petal silk into my hand and hold one to my face, and this is why people here go on living, this freshness.

I can't not smell it.

Another bunch of petals falls.

I think I see a gray rat body in the thick of the leaves' black against the dead-white sun. I unplug my ears to hear if it rustles in the leaves, and I crouch to run if it does, I do do that, I crouch out of a dream of a rat, of myself as rat. What I hear instead of rustles are giggles. I turn toward them and they're in color, I can see them: giggles that turn into Veelu, who's a branch over, giggling among others peering down from their branches.

I don't pretend I don't notice, I nod and I smile how I remember I smile. Is that Spreader? Breasts for Three? I can't say *hello*, I can't say *good-bye*.

I can't be rude.

Why do you gather so many flowers? I almost say, What a waste of time it is, all these flower crowns and leis every morning, don't you have anything else to do? Don't you have to wail and tear at your hair and not eat? But I smell the petals, the way they change what you want.

Veelu monkeys down a limb. You think we are primitive, she says.

She doesn't say this, she spits it.

I say, I don't think that.

If you have no work to do, says Veelu, you are primitive—right?

I'd say you were advanced if you don't work. I look at my hands. They are purple. Or is that the smell?

That's not what people say, she says. That's not it, not advanced.

All right, I say.

If you are primitive, you might as well be dead—that's right, isn't it? That's what people think, isn't it? Primitive means like an animal, free as an animal, easy to kill because you have nothing to do.

Maybe, out of jealousy, I say. Maybe that's why people kill.

I could run away now. I'm still in my crouch. My beach isn't far.

You are the ones who are primitive, she says. She breaks off a branch full of blossoms and points toward her belly. This is where the ghost you and your people make hurts me, she says. Six times it fills, and six times there's nothing.

That angled branch over that part of her — this is exactly the place a maid on the main island pointed her dust mop when she warned me about what on this island — sex?

No.

Veelu shrieks her *nothing,* and at the end of it comes a cry, a short, high cry, a sound I'm not supposed to hear but have to.

The other women thread their flowers.

———————————————

I keep my eyes shut against the smoke and walk into a palm. I rub my head where it hit and get into my crouch, gulping smoke in the dusk.

He comes out of the smoke, a god with a stick. Other men have their sticks, and they do a little dance in the smoke with the sticks upright, a dance men know. Then they slap each other on the back, that kind of slap, then they laugh.

They too have their names for each other, all mixed in with bits of their language and mine. Harry's I can't hear, but when it's called he struts with his stick stuck up at the groin.

But all they want is smoke! They thrust a lit stick into the base of a palm, a hole where the sand has worn away, where its root clings. Then they thrust it again into a scrub tree where a hole shows bigger. Then they do it to a tree farther down, each time waiting, sticks in hand, the hollow tree up to the man's arm, the one with the smoking torch.

And one man holds a pillowcase.

They go silent in the midst of their deflowering, except for clinical comments like *over there* or *here,* then they move on tiptoe down the beach, sticks up but wobbling, to another tree.

I follow them, using the smoke to hide behind. I don't want Harry to think I'm watching him, I don't want him to think I want to watch him. I don't want him to think about me at all. He has his women.

The man with the pillowcase trails the others. He's not far from me. It's a deflated ghost he's carrying, bunched in his dark hand. I try not to cough or to cough when he coughs. None of them knows I'm here.

At the fifth tree and after a hike, they all start to shake. They get so excited they shake and their sticks whack at the air, and then the pillowcase gets thrown down. At the seventh tree, they find what they want, but it finds a way to back off.

They light more torches that smoke. In the gloom with all their sticks, they act as one spider, all their sticks raised, the bag in the middle as a kind of globed head. They are determined now, with all their torches and sticks.

When it's finally smoked out of the hole, they catch it in the pillowcase and beat it. The meat is better beaten, someone says to Harry, but the creature inside the case fights as if it knows what is better.

Someone has already brought a pot, someone has already scooped up water from a wave, someone now sets a lit stick to a pile of sticks, and what's inside the bag is dropped into the water. Lacking a lid, the men cross their sticks over the top, they push what they've caught back into the pot.

Children chase the smoke that's left, they chase it all around me. I shiver because I don't run and shout after the smoke like they do. I want to keep on hiding.

Leaning against the tree, I hear from inside it another creature like the one they're cooking, its sound moving like the wind's inside a tree, the way the ocean sounds inside a shell. Of course I think that faint scrabbling is me, my blood inside my head, it is the kind of sound that you always think is your own, the sound of fear. And then the sound stops.

They eat it, they crack its shell, they eat more of it, the claws, they litter the beach with its pieces. There's only one for all of them, but the meat is good, very good. The children pick up the claws and chase each other through the smoke with them, they scrabble sideways, knowing how to move with that kind of claw.

A shadow fixes me. I'm already saying, What? when Harry pulls me from behind my hiding place. He brushes the sand off me. It was one of the last ones, he says without saying hello, as if he knew I was behind the tree all along.

One of the last ones? I repeat.

A nice red it turned, he says. See, there's a bit of the claw left.

The children try to bite each other with the claw.

What if you ate the last one?

I suppose you could let it die of old age, he says. There's always that. It was tough enough anyway. What's last anyway but dead?

The shells protect them, protected them from what fell.

Maybe they ate what fell, he says. Maybe that's why it was the last, or could be. Maybe that's why it was tough.

I watch the men pour a crab's worth of water from the pot into shells. No, thank you, I say when Harry offers his.

A moon rises free of the water while Harry and the others and the children pretend with their sticks to couple again with the trees, to bring forth the crabs, to give birth to them and eat them. Even the smallest of them pretends with his stick. Then—who calls them?—all of them go off.

Harry is going off too when he stops where I sit, free of the sand he has brushed from me, watching the moon and none of them, and he asks whether I can dance? He says none of the ladies he has can.

My *never* doesn't even figure, I can't even hold it in my mouth. As if I am always thinking of dancing, I take his arms, I grab hold of the ones that held the stick, the ones that beat on the last crab and then lifted the juice of its last self up to his lips in a cup, and I dance in those arms in the moonlight over the stink of the shells and the old fire.

It's a slow, slow dance, the kind sometimes you don't even lift your legs for, or turn, and sometimes you nearly fall over it's so slow. Of course I hum while he says he's not leaving here, he's never leaving here, it's his place forever.

Beseech thee, I am not lost.

Ngarima lies face down on the sand, coughing and moaning.

I beseech thee, she moans.

I sink my feet deep in the sand and study my way. And study Ngarima, yes, I must study her. It is only a little time since her son sailed off—I think. I am not sure anymore. So many nights, and if you sleep in the day covered by leaves, the days are nights too. It all gets to be night.

I am not walking anywhere when I walk here in the dark, so I walk closer, but not too close. Her grand bulk is so prostrate, her coughing so loud, those moans so hollow, like an echo off the moon. In the glow of that moon, what glows green in her hand? What hot piece of what?

Ngarima kisses that ghostly glow, then she plants it in the sand inches from her fingers, upright so it looks like it's standing.

It's a plastic Jesus. A car Jesus that glows.

Light is power, she says. She knows I'm here, I think. She coughs.

Are you all right? I ask because that's what everyone asks me.

I am fine, she coughs. Nothing is wrong. Nothing. She says *nothing* the way Barclay says *yes,* the way I say *nothing.* And you are walking? She sits up. If you walk alone in the bush, you know, a man is always walking too.

I like the moon.

She looks at its shine on her hands.

The moon is the whole island at night, she says. At night the island lives and we are ghost people. Whose eyes can see in the midday light? Then there's too much light. Light is power, isn't that what you call it? She coughs. Light is the sex of life, it is what keeps us going, light is what happens in the night to get the day to rise.

The Jesus falls over in the sand in front of her. She picks it up like it's a shell she's found, turns it over, and pockets it very fast as if I don't see. She looks up from her pocket. She says, The light that came over the island was in the day, that light, you never think again without thinking of that light, that second sun.

The palms cut the moonlight into jagged beams that sway.

She begins to sing "O Little Star of Bethlehem." Some of the words are hers, high and cracked and coughed. When she stops, she says, That was just the first star. I learned that when the army came and taught us songs.

She begins to swing her hips in dance. We take what we want of them. You see, she says, flaring her fingers, this is the star. We change the song to include that other light.

This is how we do that. She covers her face. You see, we did see. That is what we did do. Light is power, she says. She rises and stumbles forward onto the hem of her vast dress.

I move to steady her, but she backs away.

You're lost? she asks. Not to be here is lost, she says. She says, No one is lost here.

But she takes the Jesus back out of her pocket and pounds her chest with it.

I look out to sea the way an old man might, the way a Crusoe might who has not yet eaten his friend or, anyway, has not yet come to that moment of to eat or not to eat that all castaways must either physically or mentally come to, and I ask, Where is a friend?

This is a Sunday, and everyone is nowhere, they're all decked out and gone, matching flowers, bolt after bolt, all the women wrapped neck to ankle, all the men in shirts white as seacrest, gone off to that Latter Day preacher's, to his mission, the cement hut behind the flagpole that says what it says about love.

I know because I went once, in the pitch of my tourist fever when I had to divine all things island in my few days, the soul and the soup, the mean and the aberrant. I am not an every-week or even every-year churchgoer. I said to Ngarima long ago, The sea is what I worship, but now what is worship when there is no boat? No vessel, such as the son, to float out past the brimstone, to seek rest.

I'm restless.

I scratch my bites bloody, the ones that I get in the pit where the wind doesn't blow, where it's warm all night and bugs feast. I forget the bad parts while I scratch, I forget what I do every day, whether it's Sunday or not, I forget and I scratch because that's the best I can do. I scratch at my scalp, where I haven't had soap for how long? My scalp itches. I dig into the hot sand with the top of my head where it itches, I stay upside down until the itching is over, and who notices?

I let my son drain out.

The singing today is sirenlike, and the wind doesn't oppose it. I don't either, I carry it along with me, I dart from tree to tree down the beach as if they are a clef and me the music, I stand Fridayless, on a Sunday, in the lee of the song and look in.

Three rows of flowered chests swell chastely across from a row of white-dress-shirt-chested men. The missionary—I hardly know him without his helmet—climbs into the pulpit and blesses everyone, and me too, since my standing outside is not blocked by a window or screen but just waist-high pressboard over a row of cinder blocks.

I am the usual statue the congregation turns to look at when he blesses me.

I smile my smile that says, Go on.

The missionary clears his throat, he talks a long time about what the world will be like after it ends, but he mixes all of that with now. In my current state, I can't sort it out, Who are the angels after? What's the difference between this ending and the other?

Mr. Harry, is what he stops with, will you please advance?

Harry's three men in, and the others have to turn their knees to the side after he says, Oh, yes in puzzlement. He walks to the church front where the missionary's moving his big book around on his pulpit and resettling it.

The sight of Harry facing me, facing all of us, stops my scratching. I lean into the window, my jagged nails pressing into the pressboard. Other women lean into their pews, a woman waves from the back as if it is *All right* or as if it is *Honey*, and Harry is up to it: the castaway's castaway, wearing the island's starched shirt and dark pants, with a beard covering his most white features, with the rest of his skin dark and darker, but puzzled in the angle of his head, his body shifting.

You have heard the story of the apocalypse, Mr. Harry? Our text for today?

Your reverence, he says and bows his head.

The missionary sighs with satisfaction. In the apocalypse there is a reckoning, he says. More than one. And here, when some time passes, we too reckon.

Yes? says Harry.

You have come to stay with us. We are grateful for that, he says. You have come to stir the soil for us. But, he says before Harry can nod again, you must follow the Lord's laws, even the one that says a man must not know a woman other than his wife.

Harry can't find his face—the one he has is laughing, is incredulous, dismayed. I see, he says.

I am sorry, says the missionary. There is a fine.

Fine, Harry says after him. Fine?

Do you need someone to testify the truth? Do you need a witness? asks the missionary.

The congregation has some ideas about that, they murmur.

The missionary turns to Barclay before Harry can answer. Can't you hush them?

Barclay is not up to hushing them. After his son does not return, I see Barclay on the beach, even my beach, and he looks out the way I do, but the boat he wants is different. Now Barclay stares at his hands as if the missionary's quieting is cupped in them and only after that starts to rise.

But Harry says, No, no, he will pay, he does not wish the good people of this island to be scandalized further.

Not in front of your wife, says the preacher.

This is when they all turn to me. I take a step back from the window, their actual turning is such a surprise. Me? I say.

You have slept the night through with him, is this not correct? asks the small man up in the pulpit.

I begin to scratch my head hard. I knew it, I knew it.

Yes, says Harry. She says yes. Just tell me how much.

The missionary pretends to consult Barclay, who is looking out the window again to the sea, who is looking at his wife and then all around, then back to the sea. Who is nodding.

It will be five hundred dollars, says the missionary, but no interest for all the time that has gone by.

This sum shocks even the women leaning forward, this sum changes Harry from a castaway doing his duty to a citizen in outrage. What about prurient interest? asks Harry. What about greed? Harry turns to me where I am rooted. I divorce you, I divorce you, I divorce you, he says to me. That's the way the Arabs do it. Will that do? he says to the missionary up in his pulpit. Can't there just be fornication now? Or is that punishable too?

Barclay? says the missionary.

What? says Barclay.

As long as they are not pregnant you must pay, says the missionary. A kind of tax, he says. Render unto Caesar, he says. When one is pregnant, you can stop. That's how it is. We require it.

Harry begins laughing. Well, you'll be sorry to learn that if I had five hundred dollars, I wouldn't pay it. The ladies will all come to me for free.

But the congregation, especially the ladies' side of the congregation, the flowered side, makes no noise, no flurry of assent and sighs.

—·—·—·—

Two days later, I am looking for the coconuts that sometimes fall on a field where they kick balls when they have them, when I see Harry picking up rocks to make a row that stretches around the goal and on around both sides. I sit down to watch him. It's worth doing: his furred torso all muscled from picking up rocks, his arms and their flexing from putting them down. He's alone for once.

That's it, he says after he sets down another ten feet of rock. I'm fried, he says. He stirs the sand beside me to get rid of the beach crabs that swarm here and on me, some kind of crab that is too small to eat, or too successful in the sand's heat, and he sits.

I shake the hair from my face as a divorcee should, and I say, Is all this in payment?

Penance, not payment. Five hundred dollars is a lot more rocks. He draws a circle in the sand. He draws another circle.

Is this two nothings or two islands? I wonder. Or the beginning of male and female?

They don't get pregnant easily here, do they? is all I say.

Look, I can't really talk to you. Somebody checks up on me. One of the girls. They send down the very young ones now, the ones most likely to get pregnant, to try to speed things up.

I suppose my being here will increase the number of rocks you have to haul.

They come at night and put them back. He looks at me. You? You were just an excuse. You don't count. Anyone can tell you're not here. You're not here at all. You're a ghost. He holds his nose. A stinky ghost but a ghost nonetheless.

I run away, I scuttle two trees over and search for coconuts under fallen palm fronds.

Harry rises and stretches. You'll get fined too, he shouts in my direction. All those belong to somebody, you know.

I'm smacking a green one against a rock, I'm shaking it.

He repeats, You'll get fined.

Nobody owns these, I yell. But I drop this one anyway.

Just because the trees don't look planted by anybody doesn't mean they aren't anybody's property. He comes over to me, he holds me by the shoulders where I shake without the coconut.

Even the coconuts are hot, I say.

Is that what you think? says Harry. He takes his hands off me and goes over to the circles he made and brushes sand over them. You know, you sound sane, he says, just loudly enough.

I sound sane. I giggle and crab-sidle over. The way you say that with just a touch of a question, I say. How sane would you be if just breathing made you sick?

I would be crazy, he says, turning away from me. I would breathe, he says. Have babies.

Jelly babies, I say. You jerk, I say.

He goes back to his rocks. I don't know, he says, grunting and straining.

I sit in his way, on the next rock, on the next. My boat hasn't come. That's all I care about. I dig my toes into the sand so I don't fall over, so he can't move the rock, but he does. I'm dizzy, moving from rock to rock, I'm dizzy all the time now. It comes from not eating right and not too much sleep and weeping. Barclay's probably told the captain not to come back until they're all pregnant, I say.

Harry stops with the rocks. Barclay's got to get some more of that copra off his docks, he says. He would jump up and down to see the boat again. Come on, the boat probably sank.

That's not it, I say.

The sun is so far down our shadows almost touch six yards away. I look away from those shadows so close together. I get up and go to the water. I don't see it, it's only wet and then not, a warm shine on the sand. All I have to do is walk in. I'm walking in the way I have tried a few times before, to get rid of walking, to take in all that water, all that big O of an ocean, the naught of nothing, to just swallow it up and be done with it, I walk and I walk, I'm walking in almost to my neck when I walk into a bottle.

It's not mine, the one I threw, but it's close enough, some beer bottle. I catch it up and wade out, I smack it against a rock to get at the note that I see is inside.

I know it's not from him. I know that.

What is it? asks Harry. Stop crying.

He takes the note away from me. I hate this place, he reads. I hate the whole seventh grade. Signed, Sheila.

What's so sad? he asks.

I tell him.

I stop shaking when I tell him, even though I keep on crying. He holds me and holds me. Then I'm laughing, I'm leaning on his shoulder, with my eyes open and teary I start laughing, and I can't stop laughing, not even when I point, when I say, There it is, and drop the note.

It? he says. It?

—··—··—··—··— *Part 3*

The winds were headed straight at us
for days before and during the test.

Glen Curbow, former Rongerik
weather unit commander for BRAVO,
the largest of the 300 H-bombs
exploded over the Pacific

—·—·—·—·—·—·—·—

The dot is too far away to be Temu, even the way dots here mean nothing with the sky just more sea the neck bends to. Besides, Temu always floats in the lagoon. Ngarima hauls him back whenever he floats too close to the reef that his brother shot.

The dot is so far away it's like an eye test.

I don't see anything, says Harry.

Okay, so you don't. There it is, I cry. This time I point with both hands. Isn't it there?

Calm down, he says.

Big bullets of tears drop off my face and hit the sand. I turn away from the water. Sometimes, I say, I expect the sand to hiss back when I wet it.

Right. It's not that kind of hot. He looks at me a long time, and then he goes over to another big rock right where a rock would block a ball if you were kicking it that way, and he digs at it with a stick.

The sun is late. When his shadow covers the beach part of the distance between us, I tell him it's coral he's digging, it grows there, he's trying to pull out a tooth that's rooted and not rotten.

I wonder why no one's come to check on me this afternoon, he says.

It's the boat, I say. They're all getting ready for the boat.

He glances out into the dusk, where there's no light, no sign of anything anymore. Come on, he says.

He takes my hand, brushes off the sand that I have clenched in it, and leads me down the beach into the dark, step by step, slow and slower. I can smell his sweat when he catches me teetering off an outcrop. It's not here, he says. Get used to it. They tell you it's coming because they think that will make you happy.

I don't think that's why, I say. But I don't know why.

We walk along. More tiny crabs move invisibly in front of us. Things can live here, I say. We could start a pig farm, I say. Show these islanders how to raise them right.

You are insane, he says. He pulls me with his arm around my waist and then kisses me, moves his mouth over me from start to finish, sand and palm trash all over us. It is dark enough now to do that. But it is not so dark that I don't see confusion in how he looks at me—or collusion? Don't ask, he says, so I know what I've seen.

So what if I did imagine the boat, I say as we near the lagoon. I imagine my son every night, how he gets tucked into bed.

Women are always thinking of bed one way or another, he says as we round my spit. I'm sorry, he says.

My dreams are all dark.

We walk along.

In ads, all dreams are dark, I go on. Or swirly. Or at least badly lit. Good night, I say. That's how it is.

He drops me off at my hole in the sand.

Hey, if there really is a boat out there, he says, remember me in the cigarette department, okay?

I hit him hard with the side of my hand, my best fake karate.

—·—·—·—

I am on Ngarima's porch devouring the taro she put out for me, licking the tin of mackerel. She is wearing red because ghosts can't see her when she wears red and it helps her cough. I had a dream your son's boat came back, I lie to her. Ngarima is not like me, she likes to hear about her son any way she can. After I lie to her about the dream, she looks up from the taro she's mashing for Temu, she coughs and says, That boat is Barclay's.

Now I haven't looked around to check on the boat. When the sun got too bright to keep my eyes shut, I rolled out of my hole and made my way through the cool dark of the bush toward food, a simple motion, the kind I can manage. I didn't go back to where I saw that dot in the distance.

I couldn't bear to.

She doesn't say more about Barclay's boat, and Barclay's not around to ask. I'm here because if he were, then there would be no boat. But since he's elsewhere, I'm beginning to gather my hope, scattered and slow-walking away like all those small shells I tried to string.

An outboard cuts the island quiet.

Excuse me, I say, and I run, I trip over car parts, I run all the way to the end of the wharf, where I almost fall off, looking and running.

A boat, a real boat.

It's not the boat I came on. Even while it's wallowing outside the breakers I can see that, even after two months of not seeing a big boat, even after only a week's passage. But why be so particular? If I wanted a boat, this is it.

There's a staff and a snake on the smokestack. I make that out because it's the same as the one on the lighter, the boat with the outboard that now guns through the reef with its shocking roar, unearthly or at least not-of-this-island loud.

Someone in a gray suit and hood holds binoculars in the lighter, trains them toward us, a clump of islanders with bags, and me all shaggy and staring. Beside the suit with binoculars sits Barclay, who holds a parcel out of which sticks an antenna.

I turn back to run and get my stuff. I'm not fast enough, who could be that fast, with the boat waiting or going or gone?

My bag I've hooked to a twisted branch over my hole. I scoop up shorts and sand and shells and papers with my name on them and fit them in. I don't know whether that's all there is, but it's enough for the bag. I run back to the other side of the island, and I'm about to break from the bush to the wharf all out of breath, slashed raw from my run, when I see four men in gray suits, moonsuits I guess,

the kind with hoods and plastic to see out of in front, se-
curing the lighter with big mittened hands. On their moonsuited fronts these men wear big smiley faces behind white
plastic tags that turn what other color? and on their moonsuited feet they wear slumber-party slippers, the kind that
should be fluffy and pink but are smooth and the color of
rats.

The sand is sifting out of my bag onto my bare feet while the moonsuits move in their suits like figures in cartoons — even their clipboards are hard to grip with fists in gloves — when Barclay leaves them for me.

You must not get on this boat, says Barclay quickly. The boat you came on will be here soon. Don't take this boat. You must stay.

Stay? I back away, I am so surprised.

This is not the boat for you, says Barclay.

He moves as close to me as a dancer. Stay, he repeats with a smile that's threatening it's so close. I walk even farther backward, I back into the needles of a bush.

You see, we must find out exactly how bad things are here, he says, shifting his new antenna. You can go to your own doctor and tell us, he says. They won't tell us. He lifts his chin toward the moonsuits, who are now giving out handfuls of batteries to anyone who holds out a hand.

You made me miss the boat? You told Ngarima to delay me? I hold my bag tight to my front as if he is going to take it to make me stay.

That first time. He looks through a lock of his hair the way he does for women. A week here is not enough. But the boat was supposed to come back, he says, stepping in front of me to keep me as long as he can. The boat is coming back.

Should I tear out his lock of hair, scream, and run in a circle? Well, here's a boat now, I say. I start for it.

He catches me by the arm so I won't trip on a bush in front of me — so I won't run? They just make tests, he says. If you go with them, they will not let you go, they will test you and keep testing you. Our boat will come.

A few islanders line the beach's shade, ready with their bags, ready with their families.

I pull my arm away. The moonsuited men are coming toward us.

I don't like it, I say, my voice rising as if I am making a decision, as if I can with all this. I am taking this boat, I have to go home, I've got to get off this island.

You like our island? Barclay glares at me. You will not like theirs.

I wave. Over here.

Barclay lifts his arms as I walk away, as I skip over to them.

The girl who sold me the soy sauce, who's always so hot, is taking a seat next to the young woman who bore the jelly baby, who's now carrying a sandy package, and a very old man who smells like that smell from the house with all the bottles in front, and a half-dozen others get in, almost filling the rest of the boat. Ngarima's last, arriving with Temu and a small suitcase.

She has nowhere else, says Barclay, as if I have asked. I try to say, At least she has this, but Ngarima coughs hard as Barclay pries Temu off her, then Temu beats on the boat with his loose arm as she boards. When Barclay hands her the suitcase, the moonsuits push Temu's fist away, a push that rocks the boat deep.

I'll take care of her, I say.

Barclay turns his face from me.

I look to the horizon, where the big boat sits, as small as one of my son's from so long ago. One of the moonsuits radios that boat, another stretches his hand toward the lighter, gestures toward where I could sit, pats that place in fact with a *Sit here.*

What do I owe you? I shout to Barclay as they start the motor. He's barely holding Temu back from Ngarima, dollars aren't on his mind. I give him what I have, but he can't take it, Temu knocks it from my hand into the water. I bend down to retrieve it, but a moonsuit grips me by the arm, steers me onto the boat to a seat just as it jolts into gear and we're off.

It is not as if I am saved, not as I had imagined it. Sailors in angel white should have come, not men in moonsuits. An island chorus usually attends all island exits, *Barclay, I'm sorry.*

You farted, says the electronic toy the lone child sitting on the wharf presses over and over, loud with new batteries. No one's singing and dancing. A few friends of

Ngarima stand by, weeping and waving. Barclay waves, holding his package of antenna and the struggling, crying-out Temu. You'd think Ngarima was going forever, like me. In the slow circle the lighter makes as it turns away, I inspect the wharf around Barclay, where my money washes, where I spent so much time looking out to sea, wishing the boat into it. Now I wish that at least Harry stood somewhere close, up to his ankles in surf, his eyes on me.

But he's happy.

The moonsuits shoot the reef with a clumsy grinding of gears, and the lighter heaves as if the outboard won't make it, then they're hauling us up a wall of boat, a toy boat grown nightmare huge, up a long spaghetti of ladder that trails the side of the big boat and onto the deck. They haul us up with their strong arms, they shove and push and pull at us, they even put down a basket for the little girl, until we're all on board.

We stand on the deck in shock, wet with spray from the reef passage, the big boat still swaying so much you could be walking, but you're not, you don't even want to try, this is a big boat in a swell.

There is only one thing to look at. From where I stand, the island looks flat and small, almost amoeba-shaped at this angle, about to break in half and become two separate islands, mitosis, something to be glanced at under a microscope.

Welcome aboard, they say. Yes, they say when I ask about their boat going back. I like that *yes*. Then one of them slides a bracelet over my wrist with my name and birth date on it. How do they know that name and date? After the bracelet slides on, it won't come off, the snap goes tight when I pull on it.

Then they have at us, needle, calipers, and scrapers. I give them what they need, then they need more, they wave their hands, Wait a minute, there's something else, and I ask, For what? but they won't say, they wave their vials and point out urinals, they hurry us out or in.

It's important to do it fast, just off the island is what their answer suggests. Otherwise it might wear off.

I don't think so.

They want to know how many coconuts I drank or ate, and I laugh. They repeat the question. The forbidden fruit, I smile, and try to figure.

Then they lead us to the showers.

It isn't that I don't want a shower. A shower with hot water, the comfort of soap not rendered from whales or tar—or whatever the yellow cakes they sell on the island are made of—this is what I want. I'm shot straight back to all of what my place in the world counts for with that first hot spurt of water, a little more than blood-hot, laving the soap and salt off my skin under fine spray. But in the middle of the shower, the water beating on my skull releases some kind of improved thought run.

It's not as if they've given us stone soap. Too obvious.

I start to shiver under all that hot water, and I don't stop even after I dry off, even after I use their big fluffy towel on myself and I'm wrapped in it. Maybe I'm sick is what I want to think about the shivers, then I don't want to think that, not at all.

My clothes are gone. And my bag. All they leave is a gray shift and slippers.

Of course—when it's all clean, I'll get it back.

I put on their clothes. One of their smiley faces emblazons the left side of my gown. I wonder if the ones on the moonsuits were as white as this face, but I can't be sure.

Still shivering, I step out of my cubicle. I can hear the others under their showers. Somewhere farther down the long row, a man with a medical bag walks toward Ngarima's stall. I know where she is because she's wailing again. She hasn't wailed since I caught her with her plastic Jesus, but now she fills the hall with her wild, sad sound.

A sedative makes sense.

I get out of the way of that man, I walk away from him. I need to walk.

Gray metal rivets, gray stairs, no signs except "Lifeboat This Way." I skip that way. I turn toward a reindeer-and-dove-covered door on the left. I go through it, wondering at the season I had forgotten in the seasonless sway of an island. Maybe such decoration wipes time and place away, and the island is gone in a whorl of blinking light. I open the door at the top of a set of stairs, thinking this, and the island is still there, still small at such a distance, but there.

A woman comes up behind me. Can I help you, Clare?

Me? I say. I can't get used to my own name, the one everyone here knows for no reason and can say. Who are you?

Someone with you on my list. She points to a clipboard filled with names.

I see. She has a Dr. in front of her name on her tag, that entitles her to my name, the way she checks my tag.

Where am I? I ask.

The answer she gives inspires hope, to go with the insignia of snake and staff. We're a large health organization, she says.

With the UN?

Wouldn't that be nice. No, not us. I see from your records that you spent a little time on this island. What brought you here?

Nobody was going there.

She could say with a professional smile, How adventurous. Instead she says, Nobody is supposed to go there.

I guess not, I say. Why did they let me?

Some mix-up, somebody's second cousin was asleep, no doubt.

Why don't they evacuate the island?

It's not that bad, she says.

Oh, really? I smile, like her. What happened to the boat that was supposed to take me back?

Boats are always late or just a myth around here. You must be glad to see this one. The doctor moves her pens on her pen guard. Over six weeks there, wasn't it?

The boat rocks under my feet, a slight left, a slight right, and I'm uneasy to match. Over this woman's shoulder is the island, locked in incomplete reproduction. Can I make a call? I ask.

Sure. But why not get these out of the way? She turns her clipboard full of paper around. Just a couple more releases. Sign here, here, and here. She presents her pen.

I see, I say. I stare at the small print. Ngarima's wailing increases from somewhere below. I slide my foot in and out of my slipper. Do you have children? I ask her.

Not yet, she says. We're hoping. She smiles the way they do, the ones who hope.

Have you ever seen any of their babies?

She waggles the clipboard. This is my first trip out. But I've seen pictures, of course.

I nod. With her *of course,* we're in this together. Well, I say, I guess you have to have one to really appreciate those pictures.

She flattens the paper with her finger where I'm supposed to sign. You've had a very slight exposure, ma'am, she says. You should be on your way within a day or two of reaching port.

When is that?

Given the weather, it should be in three days.

I see. Three days, that's great. Where can I make my phone call?

Over there, in the poop deck.

I sign.

Hello? Hello? Hello? Hello? I start away from the cool plastic at my ear. Echo is a girl in a nymph costume, a shreddable tissue of green, who leans forward on a rock with her hands cupped to her lips, and another girl on another rock — a veritable Pacific of rocks, rocks that run right up to my ex's own cool-plastic-touched ear — leans forward with her hands cupped, and another. Every word echoes, so I must sound startled too, and strange. Does my ex notice?

I'm sorry, I say.

He turns off a radio behind him. You're what?

I never told you I was sorry.

That's true, he says. He was my son too.

Tell your wife I said so, I say.

He sighs and starts to say something, but his voice breaks.

What is it?

It's okay, he says. I forgive you.

I hold the phone and hold it tighter. It wasn't my fault, I say. It was an accident.

I forgive you, he says again.

I can't say anything.

So where are you? he asks. I called you about his savings account, but your office said you were gone.

On a boat, I say. A very strange boat, and I'm hoping it will get me to an airport. Please call my office and tell them I'll be back in a week.

There's silence on his side, an echo of silence. You still only care about work.

No—no. That never was true. You know that.

What? he says. I can't hear you.

Listen, I say, the name of the boat is—what? She told me. I lean from the booth, but she's not around to ask and there's no sign. It isn't about work, I say. Really. Tell them that on I'm this boat—

The echo girls have stopped. The echo girls sit back on their haunches and pick their teeth, bored with the actual transmission of information, and in a second I hear nothing at all from the other end, not even the insect swishing of static, of the electric wave tumbling. I say, It isn't about work at all—but the phone is already dead.

I hit the phone. I hit it again because it doesn't hurt enough the first time. I manage with number two to put myself in pain. I'm in pain, I'm in pain.

The man who lectures me, who says, That's private property, ma'am, which I understand to mean I am private property, me, the one who's in pain and hurt, not the jackass plastic, that I shouldn't be misused, that man is, say, six years older than my son was, the size my son would have been in six short years, and this baby tells me it's the only call I can make for three days and by that time we'll be in port anyway, so relax. We can't have everyone hanging on the line, he says, and maybe he pats the sucker or maybe he doesn't, but the gesture is what boys learn with machines they love instead of women. He doesn't, however, catch the way my face shifts in anger. He says, What about dinner, have you had it?

I do smell its grease, the kind that hamburger makes. After all those boiled roots and puddings, that vast pig, and those tins of fat and fish and salt and wet leather, this smell has its virtues, starting with the smell of home. Home fries, I hear him say as he herds me away from that phone. I hold my hurt hand that is all I have to remember of what I said, I wind down corridor after corridor, the smell stronger than the antiseptic, then the smell is there and the rest folds behind into memory in the presence of clicking plastic silver.

We walk in front of Day-Glo French dressing spread across equally bright greens, instant potatoes wallpaper-paste-fine topped with brown, a color that advertises a circle of meat somewhere below, ground from the tubes and ears of various short-lived creatures, all of which the server plops onto my plate in an almost musical series.

This boy I have come with touches me on the elbow to guide me past the plastic tree strung with red and gold bits of sprayed food — popcorn, macaroni, old bones? — to where the other hot ones eat. That's where he thinks I want to sit. But I have to know more than what is stamped on the faces of the left-behind islanders, the six who now, removed from the island, removed from their clothes, show their necklaces and scars above their gray wraps, their faces flat with what's been given them.

I say, Sit with me, it's been a long time since I talked to someone from home, and I see him squirm and it's all there: my exposure writ in his body's flinch, the eyes' denial that I'm a person standing in front of him, but enough like his mother that a sense of the filial lies in the way of total trashing. If only he had a video game to hide behind.

He's got his orders, he sits me at another table. But he agrees to sit nearby, he'll chat with me.

We talk islands and music and their music, as if they can't talk about their own music. But they don't want to talk about their music — or anything. The islanders barely eat. Their tests are just beginning, tests they can't pass, I am thinking, the only tests they can get. Ngarima sits in front of her food, coughing, with a look on her face that I have seen in the snapshots Temu found, a look that says, Who could eat?

Do you get to drink on board? I ask. I'm trying to sound as if I am his age or I once was and did a lot of drinking and maybe drugs too, but of course it fails. I forget my face and how surely it's hardened from a different past than his, and he gobbles another fearsome bite of his quarter-pounder with fries and says tonight is their party, it's a week early, they've got to get to the next island and the water is rough, so there won't be much drinking.

I fork through my meat and turn it over. What else? I suppose you've seen a lot of water, I say, you've probably surfed in a lot of incredible places.

He says, Yes. He brightens. Lots. And most of them look like this one, he says. He names an archipelago or two of even more far-flung islands, says the sharks are bad on some of them, but then, they glow in the dark, why worry?

He stops because his food is almost gone, because I'm staring at him, because he should. He laughs. Glow in the dark, he repeats, shaking his head at his own joke.

What if I don't test out?

Well, they'll give you a few more tests, and maybe some treatment. It's not that you want to be in any hurry not to take the tests. But don't worry, you were hardly exposed at all. Not like them. He points the chewed end of his red meat to where they sit as if they are already dead, not eating.

Where do you put the trash? I ask.

He points to a hole next to the serving area. I push in all of the brightly colored foods so they tumble into the dark that trash makes, and Ngarima comes up to me.

Don't sleep, she says. Ghosts will get you when you sleep. She looks as if she has locked her eyes again, the way you do on the island to sleep in the day.

— · — · — · — · — · — · —

Stars in absolute excess, I gulp stars in my breathlessness, swinging through the last door off the stairs that finally lead up and out, and she is sitting on the cold metal deck, her legs drawn up, her eyes on the smoke that curls but does not drift into the stillness of the star-packed air. She is a civilian now, or at least the lab coat's gone, her clipboard's stowed—nothing she holds protects her. She jerks her cup back toward her toes, away from me.

Not that I threaten her, not that I come toe to toe. I am bathing in stars. We sit in absolute dark here, an aurora borealis in reverse, black paint sucking the stars closer than even the stars on the island, which will surely someday set fire to the tops of the palms, fronds waving once too often against their white light.

'Tis the season. She offers me a shot, which I take. And I take a second one, and one more before she says it's not her bottle.

As many islands as there are stars, I say, toasting her. You like working for this corporation?

She levers herself up from the deck, weaving a little, smoothing her way forward with her feet. They give you a house at the facility, it's okay, she says. It's a very modern place.

It must be hard. I stand too.

A lot of medicine is hard. I try not to think about it.

I'm good at that.

We talk, and the dark starts to spin with words, which I try to hold on to. I ask what I need to ask, Are you the one in charge?

No.

Okay. So who is in charge? I ask.

She leans on the railing, leans as if this is why they're installed, not to keep people in but to let them lean. Below, she signals with a hand off that railing. He hardly ever comes up, not even at night. He could be in Bellevue instead of the ocean, he could be in Persia, he's a thousand-and-one-nights kind of guy. He's the one.

She's maybe more drunk than I am.

It was an accident, you know, she says.

I know what an accident is, I say.

The captain will like my story about the island, I say. In my story, children hide under it as if it were just a spoon to be overturned. But instead of being served up in a mouthful, they come up through the sand as jelly.

I stop, I go on. The important part of the story is why they are hiding.

They should hide, she says at last.

No—not children, they shouldn't, I say. What have they done?

Her smoke triples in the wait.

It's nice you don't lock us up, I say.

She dumps ash onto the deck. You're guests, you're volunteers.

Can I change my mind?

She stubs out her smoke. I say before she can answer — because yes or no isn't relevant, because it isn't my mind I want to change — See which way the palms grow on that island? Have you ever actually looked at this island?

She glances over. The island's backlit by stars. Left, she says, they grow left.

Trade winds, I say. They never blow any other way. Now, if it were all an accident, this Bravo thing, which is what the husband of the woman you have here who is screaming so much calls what happened, if it were all a big accident, if it were just a big mistake that they made, letting the cloud spew itself up, up, up and be borne by the wind, wouldn't you have to know which way it would go? Wouldn't you have looked at the palms at least? See that speck a hundred miles away, you said, that's nothing, there's just people in the way. Or maybe, Let the wind blow a little that way and then we can see what's what with a few people. Even the gravestones blew that way.

Okay, okay, she says. I didn't do it.

Did I? I ask. Before she can suck in another star off the deck or drink from her cup again, I try another voice: "Studies show that in paradise, sex is paramount, that the natives reproduce like rats" — do you hear a voice like that rising in wonder, envy, lust, do you hear it tinged with the amoral curiosity of science, some boy-scientist speaking who tears the wings off six generations of flies to see if it affects their reproductive abilities, their, you know, sex?

Our parents elected those people, I say, and we keep them in place.

She has already walked away.

The stars are still there. Hot little islands.

I stroll past a card game. The little girl from the island squats beside it. I sit down and take her on my lap, though she resists, she tries to squirm away from me in fear because I have never held her or any of them, never comforted their boo-boos or said *sorry*. At least she knows who I am, I am not the drinking woman. But of course I have no Band-Aid for her, no Band-Aid with some animal on it that children like printed on the side that's not sticky, I don't even have words she'd like to hear, *home* or *get well*, so there we struggle.

I let her go. I leave the stars for the stairs, for the very bottom of the stairs, where the doors are hot with engines behind them. Some are open, so I don't have to knock, I don't have to call out over the machines, O Captain! My Captain!

Of course, he could be sleeping. It is night, and on a boat any time is all the time, they have watches and they take turns and surely even captains sleep.

Nothing promises anything inside room after room: the machines and their couplings fill them almost to the ceiling the way plants do, a thick blooming, but one room does divide and through that burrowing division must lie its reason.

He smokes and wears a tiny hat. It's the kind you wear for building expressways or putting I-beams into buildings, but it's the wrong size, the size real estate salesmen wear when they're saying it's in move-in condition, the one that sits on the head and teeters. Despite the hat, he's in charge, he's no missionary-in-a-helmet. He doesn't bother to look up when I enter his high-tech lamp light, not even when I cast a shadow in his smoke.

He could be blind.

He is not blind enough to wear the glasses they wear because he turns to me when I say, Captain, and he blinks pale eyes, I see them see me.

Doctor, he says.

Excuse me, doctor, I say. Of course he's a doctor. That makes me fear him more, but I cast off that fear for later, when I have more time, when I don't have someone looking at me or three shots of liquor inside. I want to go back, I say.

He spreads a chart over his knees, and it caves in the middle where the blue is, where it's lined with circles inside circles inside circles. He stares at the map—to sort out the creases from the bull's-eye?

You're sicker than you think you are. But don't worry, honey, he says without looking at me. Haven't lost a patient yet. He snaps the chart taut and picks up another.

None of them? I ask.

You can think what you want, honey. He smiles at me, a dazzling smile, one with teeth, then he opens his new map, snaps that map shut. We have all the data.

He folds the map small.

One more thing, I say. Can I bum a few cigarettes from you?

He chuckles with an addict's pity and hands over what's left of his pack.

Part 4

He bolts the door behind me. I walk away slowly. He's called for security—You like security, right?—to help me find my way back. I'm to stay right there.

I start to walk away quickly. I start to climb fast, then faster when I hear someone on the stairs. It, It, is what I hear in my head, I am It. I run all the way to the rail.

It is time to choose.

A good thing it is night. By day I would think it all out, lay each piece face up and add them. At night I can't separate fear from fear. Besides, I am frightened by heights, I fear putting my head down and seeing whatever's so far down, and I can't see much but stars in this night. I still have what I drank as a comfort when I duck my head way down so when I jump it is not from a height but through all these stars.

I fall the way my son fell.

But into water.

I go so far down it feels as if I'm being pulled under by some deep-sea creature to make sure I never breathe air again. I fight my way up, and all that fight surprises me, maybe I wanted to just stay under, but I don't, I'm star-side

again and swimming. I don't think about the sharks I dis-
turb, the ones cruising the ship for its rain of leftovers, I
gasp at the top, not thinking.

Someone rimmed by the light of the stars has heard me
hit the water—she has, it could be her.

I gasp again, trying to be quiet. I'm now full of fear and
now off the boat, and now what? I'm on the dark side, at
least, where the moon isn't. I'm not going to swim back to
the island, I can't get back on the boat. I swim over and
touch the boat as if it's base.

On the island, the islanders are practicing their dancing.
I hear the clipped orders, the drums building, the tune
about holiday stars that Ngarima sang on the beach with
her Jesus. Does anyone hear me? Above, people collect
and lean over. No, nobody, is what they say about my
splash. But someone else—the woman, no doubt—says,
Yes, with such assurance that they go to find lights. That's
what they shout out to get.

What rocks in my darkness? I paddle-crawl through the
dark to find the lighter, the outboard end. I pull myself
onto it, but I am used to someone pulling me in, and it
takes me three tries plus my leg thrown over to get on.

By now lights make a plaid of the water, and I hear foot-
steps click on the ladder above the lighter. I turn the key
that's there and ready, I throttle and pull.

Boat driving is easy if you can see where you are going, if
you can at least see the gears. Otherwise you bang the boat
in reverse, you almost de-leg the man who is making his way

down to you, but all of a sudden all the light that is now on you lets you see and you go, jerking, off into the night.

You can't get through the reef in the dark, but it's not so dark anymore with all this light, all the light they need to launch another boat after yours, anyway I don't think about what I can't do, with the lighter moving so well beneath me and turning when I turn. So when the white-headed surf rears up, I find my way, I don't think of myself and the boat mangled and turned on its sharpness — I just go.

Not that I make it. The boat flips in the surf, and I capsize fast, foam and coral and some very hard wood hit me as the boat goes down. I'm senseless in a light-dark-light moment, the foam and dark sprayed into the spotlights the boat casts out for me. But when I surface, all banged up, I've been shot on a wave into the utter dark past the reef.

How can I swim? It's nothing. I do it with my legs and arms, I flail like that small-headed boy in the lagoon. When I find I can't breathe I hope to touch that soft monster sponge, but of course I don't. Did I imagine it anyway? I don't know what I do but splash and gurgle in a direction that might be forward — there — is that dark part land? Is that tin basin reflecting their light, or is it the moon? A streak of light bounces with drumming far away.

Pain comes so suddenly to my leg that it doubles me up. It must be a nail from a wreck, but next there's an electric jab into my foot so bad that I can't straighten it out, I am gone with pain, so far beyond the banging up I've just had on the reef that I take on water.

A wave, a lucky wave, tears me out of it, goes the right way, the way I think of as right where I come from, where I must go back to, a kind of amniotic wave, a slap-on-the-bottom wake-up wave that makes you cry out, outraged, and live.

—··—··—··—··—··—·

You think we didn't notice the ship all lit up and the sirens going? Harry hovers over me. A boat with horns like Jehovah blowing?

I move my head as if I might laugh with him, but no, it is impossible to laugh, I can't laugh, I can't even move my mouth very well.

Barclay saw you. What does he have to do now but walk the shore all night and wait?

What? What? I say. This is all I can say, and point at my feet, which are bandaged and itchy and hot.

You should be dead, says Harry. Or at least gone, with them, rescued as it were. What happened to you was you hit a *taramea*, a fish so poisonous we had to use gloves to pull the spines out.

A poison fish? I say, pulling hard at my mouth muscles to get to the *p*.

Harry sits on a mat beside me. I see it is his mat.

I saved you from them later, says Veelu, who leans into my vision with Milo in a half coconut.

I sip.

Show her how, says Harry. This is the saving after the fish, when they came to the island to get you back —you, their prize experiment. They swarmed the place, I thought the island would sink under their weight—or that they'd find me and take me instead.

Why didn't they? I try to say.

Veelu lifts her arms, removes a pin from her hair on top, and shakes her head. Veelu's large hair, so mane-wild and black-silked, falls off and down her back, and her own hair, the little she grows, stands in surprised wisps in small clumps over a head scarred in parallel rows. You like it? *I'm going to wash that man right out of my hair*, she sings. *And send him on his way.*

She waves the wig. They give this to my sister in a box, and it is all she has to send me. When the ship people see me without it, when they see the scars the boat has left me with, they don't bother me. You stay here too long, I say, and they'll do it to you too. They believe me when I say you are in the surf, finished.

He and Veelu laugh, and it's strange and painful for me to hear how they do it together, how he then touches her baldness with his thumb, showing that they know they look the same.

I don't know why they didn't take me, says Harry. He is quiet with old fear. He restacks the pink shells around the edge of the room. But they didn't come back, he says. Did you want to be gotten?

I am crying. The tears fill my ears and make me feel underwater again, but they are tears of relief, tears that have waited for a right time to be shed. I am not dead, I work out of my mouth.

I can smile.

I am asleep. I am not asleep. The green outside the window turns blue under my lids—or is it water coming through my head, fixing things? I am listening to the swish of palms and hurting. That's all you do when you're ill, listen and hurt, back and forth, a conversation as deep and dark as that. Sometimes a thought buzzes between them, but it can't connect to anything, can't feed off the listen or the hurt, and so it drops.

What drops? I am alone here in my sleep. I'm not at the guesthouse, I'm back on my rice bed in the house of silence—Barclay's empty house. Barclay haunts the shore, watches for what won't come in or float up, Temu making *o*'s in the water in front, in back of him.

But now something drops. Somewhere in my listening—it's a place, my listening, in my recovery—the house is vacant for me because who else will go into it, with its windmilling ghost, its lost boys and lost mother?

I am asleep, so what drops is a dove from a dream of what happened, a dove that came in a box on the Paradise shoot. Gulls were too *vulturish* to fly across the palms that were supposed to sway in a breeze from the dawn, so we had doves sent in boxes, small gray boxes, coffins, some said. When the sun finally moved out of a cloud that was supposed to be dawn's but was dusk by the time we shot, we scooped those doves out of their boxes and threw them up toward the sun.

They all dropped to the ground.

Since I am asleep, I can open my eyes.

The room is as dark as sleep. It is night. I had forgotten that, or I didn't know. When is it not night in my sleep? I could raise my hand to my eyes to see with my hand if my eyes are seeing, but my hand hurts and itches. I am too sleepy to make it rise, too tired of hurt.

The dark breathes. I breathe and it breathes. I stop and it breathes.

I could cry out. Over the pounding ocean? Over the dark, deep night in which no one else is crying? Ghost. It would be ghost, their *tupaka*. If only Barclay lay nearby, with his night noise, astraddle Ngarima with her bulk like a boat he would take out.

Or if there were just a lamp that could break.

I can see shape now. Large against what there is of a moon, the shape stands by the curtain, and its flowers quiver a little—from his entrance? From a breeze?

It is no dream, I decide. If he has not come to press himself into me, he comes to kill me, he comes to turn the pillow over on my face—or empty the rice into my nose and mouth. Because I am the one Veelu said, a Bravo person. I did it. My deciding can't stop, I hear the breathing, and I think, think, think.

I sit up. Get out of here, I shout. But what I say comes out small.

He walks into some light. Before I see him, I know. The way he walks is why I didn't wake before. I know the way he walks. It was just that dropping I didn't know.

Barclay, I say. You scared me.

He keeps on breathing. He is looking not at me but at the floor.

Barclay, I say. I slip back down so as not to feel my legs, and the slipping gives me another angle. In this angle, with light, I see Barclay's face is wet.

He's been swimming. In my pain that's what I think, then I think nothing again. Barclay's here, so what.

He's sobbing.

Thank you for saving me, I say.

His words come all at once: Ngarima was who pulled my son out of the snow that fell after, the one who died, not the one who is born later with his head, or the one who has gone away.

He steps closer to me. Radio, do you want a radio? they said. No problem. Show the others there is no problem. I will do a lot for a radio. He looks at his hands. I let my son play in the snow, to show them you could play in it, not to worry. He breathes in a sob. Oh, my Ngarima.

I was the one who wanted a radio, I say.

You are a ghost, he says. If I shut my eyes, you will vanish.

I am not dead yet, I say.

Yes, he says, turning away from me. That's what you say. You who always wants to leave this island, who calls it paradise.

Paradise, I repeat with a wave of pain. I wish I could have brought Ngarima back with me.

He stands there. You are here now, he says. He is wiping off his tears.

I watch his hands move across his clothes. Like before? I say. Like that time when you said it's the custom?

It is the custom.

I close my eyes.

He moves toward me.

Most of me is bandage-wrapped. I'm impermeable, a sweating mummy. I am thinking *impermeable* between the listening and the hurt, but when he lays his head near my arm I put my arms around him, I hold him while he cries.

Desire is as confusing as death. All the little impermeables between them switch places, get stuck. I kiss the top of his greasy hair where it is sticking up. What he wants is so big and so far from here he loses his want, he pushes it in anger against my bedside until it's drained.

I hurt. He hurts. His hurt circles his anger.

There is a machete stuck in a coconut at the door. That could be what dropped, the sound of it being stuck. But there is always some knife at the door, and what light there is is always catching on it, making it something two people will look at together.

You are going?

He's a shape again. He's moving toward the door.

I will tell Harry to move me. You want your house back, that's it, isn't it? I say.

Barclay opens the hands he's kept clenched. They take hold of the wavering flower cloth at the door and they tear it down, one long rip against nails.

Then he's gone.

Bare feet don't make steps that dwindle, and nothing thuds or sways or whistles behind him. The new stars the cloth kept dark are all I have to know I am awake.

I am awake now.

_ ._ ._ ._ ._ ._ ._ ._ ._ ._ ._

There's little blond left, I have a bad limp and a crutch, I have pale brown skin from the sun bouncing off my sheet, with its heat on the wall behind me that I feel on my back sitting up straight on my rice bed, which is now so thin.

I sit up so straight now that I could receive radio waves myself or at least intercept them, have the radio play in my fillings, hum out that the boat is coming, the real boat. The radio, declares Barclay when he visits, says a boat is coming, he has his antenna that lets him talk. He can *yes* me now.

Barclay lingers after he tells me about the boat. I catch and hold his hand. I say, You think I'm not grown up, that I think sex is all that matters to you?

You will find someone, he says.

This is a compliment I think I can take. But he doesn't say more. He walks away quickly to radio again, to talk more about all that I have told him about that other boat. He disappears very fast since my angle for seeing isn't far. He just disappears.

At the highest heat of the day, Clam Hold and Breasts for Three come to string white flowers onto fishline at the end of my bed. They laugh over the penis-shaped buds that turn up—but their laughter is not envy the way some would say. And they do not say, What's with that man now?

Harry doesn't pick up rocks anymore. He tells me he doesn't have to. I've done it, he says. To whom is not clear. In this climate, buds burst on cues I can't sense. That is, all these flowered cloths billow loose, all these women leave their shoes outside his house, and others. But only Veelu runs down his shoes now, smokes his last all-dried-out cigarette.

The two women wreathe me in white flowers. What's this? I say.

Nothing bad, says Clam Hold, if that's what you mean. It's just that you smell like water that sits. She pulls another layer over my head.

I used to steal coconuts, I say as I sniff the buds.

You used to be crazy, says Breasts for Three. Or a baby. Wanting to drink that hot milk instead of him.

They really laugh now.

Have I made them up? Thick-limbed with coarse skin, wide hands, and scarred necks, they have names but don't use them, they have children but can't keep them.

Clam Hold tells me it is the end of Christmas week, but those aren't quite bells I hear out the window—two machetes banging into each other. All men into their houses is what that clanging means, she says. No one's coming to gut and roast me.

Here is the needle, Breasts for Three says. She gives me the long, sharp tool for stringing flowers. You can finish these. She heaps the rest of them into my lap. You Old Coconut, she calls me as they leave, as they rush off.

An old coconut is coconut through and through, no milk, no slick fruit, sweet but inert and dry. They leave me to go roaming. Today—once a year—despite the Milo missionary and these flowered cloths that conceal so much— the men stay inside the houses and all the women switch.

But I am the Old Coconut.

They know my boat is coming, that radio has me already boarding it.

Say you stay with one man but another one wants you, but not forever. How can you know how long that is? Is that tomorrow, or is that until you die and take time, its long fall, with you? Or is it just for Christmas? Imagine how that man will try to impress you here. This is no ritual rape, this is contest. The men cook, they keep food out at all times. I can hear one sing how much coconut oil he has to rub in.

It's so warm today I take off my shirt and doze, still wreathed. These flowers are not meant to go into a cooler and be kept. They must be crushed and worn, their scent released. A bee wakes me, checking the folds on the buds that have opened. He is so anxious, burrowing in. Does he look for another bee and not food? Has he lost love?

Christmas and children.

I shake myself awake. I remember my shirt and its heat, but I pull it on anyway, pull up the flowers to settle my shirt under them. I am no South Pacific maiden. I lean out for my crutches, a fresh set made from y's of wood, all the prickles planed or sawed off, the two stumps almost level, and it's then that I see the loose flower.

It's bruised and brown in its creases and sweet-scented like the others, but all its petals have grown lopsided, every petal hooks to the center, but every petal on it is different, defective, unmatching, then every petal falls soundlessly to the floor between my fingers as I hook them off the middle with effort, pulling them apart so they're no longer confused, no longer growing wrong and bad.

He loves me, he loves me not.

Shush, shush, go the grass skirts on the women.

I gather myself on the crutches.

I go to find a house.